Praise for *Ma*

"The desire to serve clients often leads to agencies trying to do it all. *Market of One* addresses this challenge with valuable lessons on building a distinct vision, culture and offering. For leaders ready to escape the industry's 'Big Grind' and drive sustainable growth, this is an essential read."

Dimi Albers, Global CEO – Dept

"As an agency search consultant with a quarter century of experience, I wholeheartedly endorse *Market of One*. This book offers a transformative approach to the agency landscape, emphasizing the importance of true differentiation and empowering leaders to reclaim their unique value. With actionable insights, it serves as a call to action for anyone ready to revitalise their agency and thrive in today's challenging environment."

Lisa Colantuono, President – AAR Partners

"Full of optimism and written with deep affection for agencies, *Market of One* offers an actionable antidote to empty positioning statements, low margins and the daily pressures of agency life."

Ete Davies, EVP EMEA – Dentsu Creative

"An articulate treatise on what ails many agencies today, *Market of One* deserves a place on the bookshelf of agency leaders everywhere."

Blair Enns, author – The Win Without Pitching Manifesto

"To survive new threats to revenue and growth, agency CEOs need to distinguish themselves from their commodity competitors. *Market of One* takes a much needed swing at traditional agency positioning. Instead of lauding their 'creativity' or desire to be client 'partners', agencies need to become unique solvers of business problems."

Michael Farmer, author – Madison Avenue Manslaughter and Madison Avenue Makeover

"Agencies correctly preach that strategy is sacrifice, but most find this principle problematic. Part manifesto and part manual, *Market of One* explains 'why?' and then 'how?' agencies can cut through and earn a premium. It's a timely roadmap towards a better-differentiated and better-remunerated marketplace."

Lawrence Green, Director of Effectiveness – Institute of Practitioners in Advertising

"The best way to beat the competition is to not have any – to find a space no-one else can occupy. *Market of One* is a roadmap to get your agency to that rarefied place."

Greg Hahn, Co-Founder – Mischief @ No Fixed Address

"Refreshingly honest, optimistic and free from corporate fluff, *Market of One* is a witty and future-focused guide to carving out your own space – no matter your agency size. Packed with relatable experience, it goes beyond theory to offer actionable insights on the power of agency individuality. *Market of One* is a must-read for any leader."

Cat Harris, Head of Talent Development & Inclusion – IPG Mediabrands

"*Market of One* demonstrates how strategic focus creates more demand, more control, and more profit. This is both a call-to-arms and a roadmap for agencies wanting to transition from dispensable commodity player to sought-after premium partner."

John Harris, President & CEO – Worldwide Partners Inc.

"Cutting through the usual bollocks about agencies and their 'secret sauce', *Market of One* is the timely, optimistic and essential alternative that our industry is crying out for. If you want your agency to leave a dent in the universe, read this book."
 Nils Leonard, Co-Founder – Uncommon Creative Studio

"I wish I'd had this book 20 years ago – it would have saved countless hours and not a few headaches. *Market of One* is necessary reading for any agency leader who's ready to do the hard but essential work of creating a lasting competitive advantage."
Michael Lebowitz, Founder & Executive Chairman – SPCSHP

"Rarely have I read a more clear-eyed, gut-punch state of the union than *Market of One*. But it's more than just a sharp diagnosis of our industry, it's also that rarest of things – a manifesto streaked with practicality; a blueprint for genuine differentiation for those brave enough to take the plunge."
 Conrad Persons, President – Grey London

"The only book worth reading if you're serious about growing your agency. *Market of One* patiently and expertly decodes just what it takes to give yourself an unfair advantage."
 Richard Robinson, Executive Director – Ingenuity+

"A much-needed jolt for agencies who have fallen into the sameness trap, *Market of One* is a practical and inspiring guide to building a business that's genuinely differentiated. If you're serious about growth and tired of playing the pitch-and-hope game, start here."
 Bill Scott, CEO – Droga5 London

"*Market of One* somehow manages to hold up a mirror to the challenges we all face in 'agency land', while making it our idea to get out there and do the things we know we should be doing, but all too often don't. The hope and optimism are inescapable."
 Toby Southgate, Global CEO – We Are Social

"'Physician, Heal Thyself!' *Market of One* is a long overdue challenge to why an industry which prides itself on differentiating its clients' brands is so averse to differentiating its own."

Rory Sutherland, Vice Chairman – Ogilvy

"Pulling no punches, *Market of One* skewers the 'dog ate my homework' excuses and forces agency leaders to take a long look at where their responsibility sits. It's honest, direct and reflects the reality that a thriving business isn't just about financial results – you need to enjoy what you do and bring your talent on the journey with you."

Sam Theobald, Chief People Officer – Next 15

"*Market of One* is an overarching study on the agency sector's challenges and opportunities, as well as an actionable guide for leaders looking to position their businesses for sustained relevance and growth in a busy, dynamic market."

James Townsend, CEO – Stagwell EMEA

"One of the great ironies in agencies is that they sell strategic targeting and differentiation but tend to commoditize themselves by claiming to be everything for anyone. *Market of One* is a recipe for the modern agency that wants to stand out and grow."

Faris Yakob, author – Paid Attention;
Co-Founder – Genius Steals

"If leading your agency feels like wading through treacle, *Market of One* will help you recover your inspiration. It's a framework for you and your team to set a vision and strategy that can elevate and truly differentiate your business. I wish I'd read this 30 years ago when I started in agency management."

Stephen Woodford, CEO – Advertising Association

MARKET OF ONE

How your agency can rewrite the rules and create a lasting competitive advantage

ROBIN BONN

First published in Great Britain by Practical Inspiration Publishing, 2025

© Robin Bonn, 2025

The moral rights of the author have been asserted.

9781788607360 (hardback)
9781788607377 (paperback)
9781788607384 (epub)
9781788607391 (mobi)

All rights reserved. This book, or any portion thereof, may not be reproduced without the express written permission of the publisher.

Every effort has been made to trace copyright holders and to obtain their permission for the use of copyright material. The publisher apologizes for any errors or omissions and would be grateful if notified of any corrections that should be incorporated in future reprints or editions of this book.

EU GPSR representative: LOGOS EUROPE, 9 rue Nicolas Poussin, LA ROCHELLE 17000, France Contact@logoseurope.eu

Want to bulk-buy copies of this book for your team and colleagues? We can customize the content and co-brand *Market of One* to suit your business's needs.

Please email info@practicalinspiration.com for more details.

Dedication

For Lily and Gracie – build a rocket, girls.

TABLE OF CONTENTS

INTRODUCTION: The promise 1

PART ONE: Adapt or die 9
   Chapter 1: Beyond the Oversupply Myth 11
   Chapter 2: The Big Grind 29
   Chapter 3: Six reframes for modern leaders 49

PART TWO: Five principles for creating your
Market of One 69
   Chapter 4: Your recipe for competitive advantage 71
   Chapter 5: Principle 1 – Believe in Better 77
   Chapter 6: Principle 2 – Define your Dream 83
   Chapter 7: Principle 3 – Craft your Narrative 103
   Chapter 8: Principle 4 – Walk the Walk......................... 133
   Chapter 9: Principle 5 – Reap the Rewards 153

PART THREE: Choosing to thrive 187
   Chapter 10: Address the hurdles 189
   Chapter 11: Bring people with you 199
   Chapter 12: Enter the promised land 205

Appendices 209
   Resources 211
   Further reading 215
   Acknowledgements 219
   About the author 223
   Index 225

INTRODUCTION:
The promise

> 'If you don't change direction, you may end up where you're heading.'
> *Proverb (origin unknown)*

Running an agency can be joyful, fulfilling and lucrative. But for too many leaders it's become an unforgiving grind.

This has to change.

In recent decades, the agency market has become a crowd of lookalikes. Trading on services is no longer a viable means of differentiation. And even if your agency is objectively better, your statements of quality are lost in the noise of lesser voices claiming the same.

At the same time, agencies are running lean and being compelled to do more for less. You're also facing in-housing, fewer retained relationships, shorter client tenures and more frequent repitches. And now Artificial Intelligence (AI) is automating vast swathes of billable hours.

In this context, only the very best maintain an upward trajectory. The undifferentiated majority are wrestling with slow top-line

INTRODUCTION: The promise

growth, depressed profits and a stifling inability to hire, retain and motivate great people.

The consequences of all this are not good. Depending on your size, according to 2023 research from the American Association of Advertising Agencies (4As) and the Association of National Advertisers (ANA), each lost pitch wastes hundreds of thousands of pounds or more. You're also leaving millions on the table in untapped organic growth. And replacing top talent costs tens of thousands of pounds while disrupting fragile client relationships.

If left unchecked, at best these dynamics handcuff you to an exhausting treadmill. At worst, your agency will cease to exist.

Clearly a new approach is essential.

Change is in your hands

Whether your business identifies as an agency, a consultancy, a studio or something else, your various trade bodies and industry communities can only help so much. Real change comes from within.

That's why this book is as much about optimism as it is about practical change. It empowers you to take charge of your future by reasserting your right to be paid well for a job well done. And because your time is precious, let's cut straight to the big reveal:

> **The agency market isn't oversupplied, it's just under-differentiated.**

Believing the former makes you a hostage to fortune. Embracing the latter means you can change the world.

This reframe illuminates the road ahead. Just because there are countless agencies doesn't mean you can't stand out. And once your ideal clients see you as meaningfully different, everything changes. You earn the right to sell differently, which creates the opportunity for you to price differently and transform your commercial performance.

This liberates you to focus on the work that excites you, be handsomely rewarded for the impact you create, and become a beacon for the best talent around. It's how you stop agency life being a grind.

And guess what? None of this is possible by trying to be all things to all people. I mean, who knew?

So how *can* you do it?

Owning your Market of One

To thrive in this densely-packed market and consistently sell your work at a premium, your only option is to harness what makes you genuinely different. Uniqueness is absolutely possible – but only once you know what to look for.

By combining your experience, culture and beliefs, you can design a unique offering that your competitors simply cannot match. This sets you apart in a space that you can truly own.

This is your 'Market of One'.

To create this modern, industrial-grade differentiation, you can't rely on a pithy strapline. Creating your Market of One isn't about packaging – it's your business strategy. You need to carefully design your agency as a robust solution to your ideal client's most pressing problem.

This business-wide client-centricity is transformational. Clients will reward your focus with their business, their loyalty and their respect. Lead generation ceases to be endless door-knocking. Pitching becomes an act of energizing co-creation. And your client relationships evolve from uneasy power-plays to genuine partnerships.

INTRODUCTION: The promise

What to expect

Part manifesto and part how-to guide, this book is for leaders at all levels, regardless of the size, ownership and core discipline of your agency.

It's designed to make you think and then support you through change. Only by seeing the severity of the issues will you be ready to adopt the practical solutions. First you regain traction, then you take action.

So, to apply the classic maxim of *'tell 'em what you're gonna tell 'em, tell 'em and tell 'em what you told 'em'*, here's what you can expect.

Part One begins with some difficult truths. And fair warning, I don't pull any punches. It's important you appreciate just how dark things have gotten. Then you'll find six liberating reframes to light your path as you find your way out.

Part Two is a practical guide to creating your Market of One. Here you'll find five essential principles to adopt and live by:

1. **Believe in Better**: Master your own destiny
2. **Define your Dream**: Harness the motivational power of clarity
3. **Craft your Narrative:** Develop a focused strategy
4. **Walk the Walk**: Make your points of difference real
5. **Reap the Rewards**: Drive profitable growth.

With any luck, these principles sound energizing or at least intriguing. Each one builds on your existing strengths. Creating your Market of One doesn't mean tearing everything down and starting again. I mean, who's got time for that?

Finally, Part Three is 'Choosing to thrive'. This is about action. It acknowledges that to create your Market of One, you'll need to bring people with you, make the case for change and address whatever's in the way.

INTRODUCTION: The promise

A new mindset

Before you dive in, I want to emphasize something. Just now I said that this book is about 'optimism and empowerment'. Don't just gloss over that – like, yeah that sounds *nice*.

Business change and personal change must go hand-in-hand. Any lasting improvement in agency performance relies on you upgrading your beliefs and behaviours.

Why does that matter? Because for all its positive bluster, much of the agency sector is riddled with fear. Whatever confidence it has is wafer-thin and just as brittle. In truth, most agencies are now indistinguishable other than by price. By definition, you're in a commoditized market.

And here's the kicker. Your commoditization is self-imposed. To quote Radiohead: 'You do it to yourself, you do. And that's what really hurts.'

That's why alongside the practical guidance, this book also invites you to upgrade your mindset – from one of scarcity to one of abundance. Once you stop fearfully following the unwritten rules, you're liberated to chart your own path.

Until then, you'll keep routinely blaming your woes on clients, on procurement and on the market. Driven by a fear of not having enough, you'll keep pitching for everything, giving ideas away and slicing your fees. But these aren't unavoidable costs of doing business – they're just choices. The glorious reality is that you get to decide.

To step into this new world of self-belief, reject just trying to win enough to keep going. Instead, focus on creating the kind of agency you've always aspired to work in.

If that sounds idealistic then I'm glad. It's a measure of the size of the prize. And if it feels like a risky pivot, just remember that when you're adrift in a sea of sameness, the real risk is to go

INTRODUCTION: The promise

with the flow. That's why creating your Market of One doesn't require a leap of faith – you just need a leap of imagination.

Is this book for you?

In case it's not clear, this book is for the open-minded. But if you're still unsure whether to read on, let me offer some context.

Prior to founding Co:definery in 2016, I spent a long career in agencies large and small; from start-ups and global networks to indies on a journey to exit. Across a wide range of agency disciplines, my role was at the sharp end of commercial success, running growth teams of all shapes and sizes. Over the years, I led successful pitches for brands including Ford, Facebook, Procter & Gamble, Spotify and Microsoft.

As I became more senior, I was increasingly hired in more transformational roles. My brief was often similar: to help evolve, revive or otherwise redirect the agency. In each case, the CEO recognized that meaningful change needed to be commercially driven. New proposition, new go-to market plan, new way of selling, new client types and so on.

Needless to say, some of these transitions were more successful than others. My biggest learning was that change only sticks when it's backed up with real conviction. No amount of fanfare for a new strapline can make up for a lack of strategic rigour or organizational buy-in. Success requires substance, as well as tangible progress along the way.

I also learned that changing an agency's fortunes isn't some unattainable pipe dream, reserved for the best of the best. Although unrealistic expectations and toxic habits will always hamper progress, once those hurdles are cleared, a new future is always possible.

In short, I consistently found that any agency with clarity and commitment can blossom into a thriving business, where everyone feels energized and fulfilled by their work, their clients and their take-home pay.

Over the subsequent years since launching Co:definery, my conviction has only grown. We've advised close to 150 agencies and coached dozens of senior leaders, working with global networks, like DDB, McCann and BBDO, as well as plenty of major indies and small unknowns. Regardless of scale, ownership, discipline or geography, the problems are clear, consistent and urgent. And I've seen more than most how different philosophies, models and mindsets play out.

The bottom line is that I've yet to meet a single agency that doesn't have at least the potential to create their own Market of One.

So is this book for you? That's for you to answer. At the very least, you'll find a challenging Point of View that combines an outside perspective with a whistleblower's candour.

Written with kindness

Finally, forgive me three disclaimers.

The first is about generalizations. Although there are consistent similarities between the majority of agencies, there's also endless variation – not least in structure, leadership and revenue models.

From global holding companies, right down to small independents living hand to mouth, some agencies are fuelled by retainers, others by projects, with plenty seeking a blend of both. Likewise, a founder's remit is different to that of a CEO in a holding company shop, which is different again to the leader of an agency backed by private equity.

Referencing this matrix of nuance throughout would make this book unreadable. So please consider all generalizations to be an act of kindness. If anything jars, I apologize. The ideas

INTRODUCTION: The promise

in this book are designed to be consistently relevant but must be applied with care. Where relevant, I've called out important distinctions. Otherwise, I leave that to your discretion.

The second disclaimer is about the use of named examples. Although this book is full of real-world reference points, often the agencies are anonymized. First and most obviously, referring to Co:definery clients in any detail would breach their confidentiality. Perhaps more importantly, as you'll read, your journey to creating a Market of One is unique to you. It's all about your ownable points of difference. So your motivation – as well as your raw materials – should come from within.

My final disclaimer is more personal. This book is my love letter to the industry that's given me so much over the first 25 years of my career. But despite being about optimism, there's a fair bit of exasperation in here too. Unfortunately, kick-starting a better future does require a punchy reality check. So please listen out for the underlying affection. Every poke in your ribs comes from a good place.

My hope is that this book makes you smile, think and act. Running an agency might be your passion, your livelihood and your identity, but it's not exactly life and death. I mean, come on – this shit's supposed to be fun.

That's why I do this work every day. Clients *need* strong agencies. And agency people are amazing. You're positive, resourceful and innovative. Once the shackles come off and you operate from a position of power, you absolutely can change the world *and* enjoy the journey.

It's time to get you, your agency and this whole bonkers industry back to rude health, feeling focused, reinvigorated and fulfilled.

Let's do this thing.

R.B.

PART ONE:
Adapt or die

Chapter 1:
Beyond the Oversupply Myth

Let's start with a question: Which agency is the best of the best right now? In any given discipline or region, there's always at least one, but rarely more than two or three.

Who is it in your space?

This is the agency who can apparently do no wrong. They win more clients. They get the best briefs. They dazzle from conference podiums and the pages of the trade press.

Not only that, but their work is consistently impressive and they're growing like crazy, even if everyone else seems to be wading through treacle. It's like they're playing to a different set of rules.

Here's another question. If you asked your colleagues the same question about who's smashing it right now, would they come up with the same answer as you?

They probably would. Such is the nature of the agency space. There are the elite – and then there's the rest. There are very few places on the podium.

This truth is reinforced whenever I ask these questions from the stage at an agency conference. Regardless of the country or the size of the audience, they soon reach a friendly consensus about who's at the top of any given tree.

And that's where it gets interesting.

How the best agencies thrive

My follow-up question – for you, as well as for conference attendees – is much harder to answer: What do you think these agencies are doing differently?

Here the responses are many and varied. Easy conviction is replaced by more of a brainstorming vibe. Answers are offered, not stated. Vocal inflections reveal uncertainty.

There's often some envy – all this success must be down to luck or connections. Others jump to subservience: 'Oh, they're just uniquely talented, they have better people, they're better known than we are.'

With a little bit of digging, the suggestions get deeper. These agencies are braver, more innovative or more able to invest. They're better at pitching. They're more focused and specialized. They serve a growing market.

In short, no-one actually knows what the best agencies are doing differently. There are plenty of ideas, many of them valid. But there's no consistent view on what it takes to thrive.

And therein lies the point. If you run an agency and don't have a robust and tailored plan for success, then you won't get close to your potential.

So where should you start?

Your market's not oversupplied

Having been doing this a while, I'm happy to report that when it comes to agency growth, the biggest game-changer is available to everyone – it's your mindset.

The majority of agencies carry the burden of feeling like they're one of many. And of course it's a seriously crowded market. But that's only a problem if you all look the same.

The reality is that, far from being oversupplied, the agency market is actually just under-differentiated. Recognizing this distinction is fundamental to your success.

As long as you believe that your market is oversupplied, you're taking your clients at face value when they tell you they can get exactly what you offer from any number of alternative shops – all of whom, they say (often correctly) will gladly offer it for less.

Now, obviously clients will tell you this to strengthen their own hand. But once you understand their tactics, you can see past the fiction of 'oversupply' and empower yourself to be treated differently.

The dark art of supplier conditioning

Belief in what I call the 'Oversupply Myth' has become endemic. The combination of canny client tactics and agencies' inability to resist has enshrined an artificially unlevel playing field.

Are you aware of 'supplier conditioning'? If you're not, you should be. It's the deliberate weakening of your negotiating position. And it's not limited to pricing conversations – all aspects of your client relationships are fair game. From opaque buying criteria and unspecified shortlists, to unknown budgets, ridiculous deadlines and undertones of dissatisfaction, these tactics are designed to exploit your neediness. The more uncertain they make you, the more pliable you become.

Interestingly, this can work both ways. Agencies often forget that sellers can condition buyers too. You'll read more about that in Chapter 9.

For now, be aware that clients consistently curate and overstate their bargaining power. And by accepting that it's 'just the way it is', you're sleepwalking into a position of weakness. You're placing yourself at the mercy of those who seek to pay you as little as possible. Unsurprisingly, that doesn't end well.

Thankfully, there's good news. Because the Oversupply Myth is just propaganda, its impact relies on your unquestioning consent. And that means you have a choice.

So you're now standing at a fork in the road to success. If you're a fan of the movie *The Matrix*, this is the classic 'red pill or blue pill' moment. Do you believe the Oversupply Myth? Or do you want the truth?

Don't default to commodity

Taking the blue pill sustains the status quo. Sadly, seeing the market as oversupplied is very much the well-trodden path. It's also the path of pain. If you believe that your agency offers only what others can, then you're implicitly committing to commoditization.

To be clear, being a commodity means being indistinguishable other than by price. Read that again, indistinguishable *other than by price*. That really should raise your hackles – it's no way to run a company (I did promise some punchy truths – remember it's coming from a good place).

Perhaps you're thinking, 'how dare you!', mentally crafting a passionate rebuttal that speaks to your agency brand, your awards or your people. But be honest, is your defence any different to the generic hyperbole that agency leaders have trotted out for decades? You can quaff the corporate Kool-Aid and claim to be unique, but your agency isn't different just because you say it is.

Don't believe me? Ask your clients what they hear agencies claim as points of difference. It's like an echo – the same sentiments, repeating into nothingness. Your voice lost in a chorus of conformity.

The commercial reality of commoditization is no fun. From slow top-line growth and pressure on margins, to a constant battle to hire and retain talent, agency issues all stem from a failure to be seen as meaningfully different.

And if you do believe – tacitly or otherwise – that oversupply *is* just the way it is, then you're complicit in the most disheartening frustrations of running an agency. Do any of the following feel familiar?

- Pitching too much and winning too little
- Loss-leading initial projects not leading to higher margin work
- Inability to convince clients to do more innovative work
- Believing that clients hold all the cards (and feeling unable to challenge them)
- Searching for a magical strapline that creates differentiation
- Struggling to make your credentials stand out
- Lead generation being a constant challenge
- Needing to give procurement their 'pound of flesh'
- Lack of senior client face time.

I could go on, but you get the idea. In fact, you could probably write your own list. These symptoms of so-called oversupply are very real. They're what you're choosing when you don't believe that your agency can be truly different.

You're cultivating a passive mindset where life happens to you, not for you. Such is the negative impact of the Oversupply Myth.

As you'll read in Chapter 2, this creates all manner of self-perpetuating roadblocks to success. That might not sound like an appealing read, but it's essential. Once you see these issues,

PART ONE: Adapt or die

you can't unsee them – and you'll have taken your first step to solving them.

For now, take a breath, grab a coffee and get comfortable. The blue pill wasn't much fun, so let's see where the red pill takes you instead.

The path of genuine difference

Choosing the truth takes you to a different future. Instead of languishing as one of many, what if you could own your category?

This is entirely achievable. Everything changes once you're seen as genuinely different. Winning great clients becomes easier, you're able to charge what you're worth and amazing talent forms an orderly queue at your door.

To illustrate the profound impact of uniqueness, let's consider the bottled water market. Imagine you're thirsty. You walk into a convenience store and you're confronted with dozens of brands; rows of transparent bottles with predictable images of springs and mountains.

Fortunately, there are a few subtle differences to help you decide. Some come in big bottles, others are small. Some are sparkling, others are still. Some have brands you recognize, others are generic. There's also a helpful spread of pricing against which you can gauge the value of quenching your thirst.

The point is that water is water and your choice is subjective – it all boils down to preference. Maybe you don't trust the cheap brands. Perhaps one sponsors your favourite sport. Whatever. You pay, you drink, you move on.

And so it is with agencies. Similar packaging, indistinguishable services and variable price points. So clients make their decisions based on personal criteria and constraints. I don't know about you, but right now, running an agency sounds about as appealing as launching a new water brand.

And then along came Liquid Death.

In case you're unfamiliar, Liquid Death is water. And that's where the similarities to its competitors end. Just seven years after launch, Inc.com reported that it was worth $1.4 billion. And no, 'billion' is not a typo.

This colourless, flavourless liquid is literally the same as dozens of alternatives in what is – *ahem* – a saturated market. And yet, by carving out their own unique, defendable space, they've successfully created a 'unicorn' brand.

Their narrative blends worthiness with joyful insanity. They describe Liquid Death as an evil plot to make the world healthier and more sustainable. With their novel packaging – cans, not plastic bottles – and heavy metal, energy drink aesthetic, they look, feel and sound like no-one else.

As Andy Pearson, Liquid Death's VP of Creative told me when I bumped into him at a conference: 'When everyone else says the same thing, that's the best possible brief to create a category of one.'

I'll drink to that, Andy.

Lessons from unicorn agencies

Liquid Death's success demonstrates what's possible when you truly believe that you offer something different – even if your core product is the same as everyone else's.

It's the same in the agency space. As mentioned earlier, your capabilities are probably pretty similar to those of your competitors. But that doesn't mean you can't redefine your category.

PART ONE: Adapt or die

Get uncommonly clear

Following a remarkable run of growth in their six years since launch, the UK-based creative agency Uncommon Creative Studio sold a controlling interest to the French holding company Havas. *Campaign* reported that the deal was worth up to £120 million. That's pretty decent progress.

Even if you don't know the UK market, it won't surprise you to hear that when Uncommon was founded, the world didn't need another advertising agency. Just like it didn't need another bottled water brand.

Uncommon launched with an explicit intention to *build brands that people in the real world actually wish existed*. This conviction has guided all their decisions, including the work they do, the investments they make and the brands they work with.

When one of Uncommon's founders, Natalie Graeme, guested on Co:definery's podcast, 'The Immortal Life of Agencies', she said that they consciously 'choose which brands we make famous'.

Take a moment to feel the confidence in that phrase. Imagine the mindset it engenders in Uncommon's people. How do you think it shows up in their work and their client relationships? I doubt they're wrestling with powerlessness commoditization.

No guts no glory

Here's another example, Miami-based advertising agency, Gut. Now, I've been to a fair few editions of the annual Cannes Lions International Festival of Creativity, but I've never seen a reception like the one afforded to two of their co-founders, Anselmo Ramos and Gaston Bigio, as they took to the stage in June 2024.

The atmosphere was electric – more concert than conference. Despite being the last day of Cannes, the main stage in the

Palais was packed. People were wearing Gut t-shirts. And when Anselmo and Gaston appeared, the place went crazy.

They were there to share how they founded Gut just a few years before, how they'd won the previous year's Cannes Independent Network of the Year award, and how they'd gone on to sell a majority stake to global technology company, Globant.

They pitched it beautifully – all swagger, zero arrogance. They stayed humble, thanked their loved ones and shared the credit with their colleagues. There were no outlandish claims. No suggestion that their 'creativity' was somehow magic. No supernatural 'secret sauce' that mere mortals can only dream of.

In fact, the 'secret' was right there in their talk's title: 'Don't Start an Agency, Start a Brand.' Gut knew it was essential to be different from day one:

- They defined their ideal client and said no to the rest (they declined 27 briefs in their first year)
- They shared their ambitions publicly and pursued them with intensity
- They built their entire business strategy around who they wanted to be.

In short, they got super clear and then they committed to making it happen. There are many talented agencies out there, but few commit to creating a differentiated brand. Most settle for surface-level distinctiveness – tweaking their packaging to tease out marginal differences.

Just like Uncommon in the UK, Gut was born out of another supposedly 'oversupplied' agency market in the US. No-one was saying 'you know what this market needs? Another creative agency'. But they showed up with conviction, went stratospheric at speed and rightly became the envy of their competitors.

Can your agency be a unicorn too? It absolutely can. As long as you recognize that your market's not oversupplied, it's just under-differentiated.

This means believing in yourself enough to challenge the outdated orthodoxy of how agencies grow. Forget how many competitors you think you have – or even how similar they seem. Instead, remember what Andy from Liquid Death said a few pages back: 'When everyone else says the same thing, that's the best possible brief to create a category of one.'

What is a Market of One?

From the dispiriting grind of 'oversupply' to the rocket-fuelled success of the best agencies around, the contrast couldn't be more compelling.

You can reject powerless commoditization by creating your own Market of One. Being in a Market of One means becoming the obvious choice for certain clients when they're facing a certain challenge. You're the leader in a category defined by your own expertise.

This could be literally anything – narrow or broad – from supercharging iconic brands to helping start-ups secure funding.

You become the *obvious* choice when what you offer is unique. Your competitors probably have the same *capabilities*, but applying your experience, culture and beliefs is what makes your agency tangibly different for the clients that matter.

In short, you have a clear and lasting competitive advantage.

Creating your Market of One has little to do with straplines, missions or heritage. It's not about fancy copywriting, trademarked buzzwords or insipid clichés about people being your 'most important asset'. And it certainly isn't about reeling off a long list of capabilities or trying to be all things to all people.

Instead, you need a robust business strategy, based on genuine conviction about who you are and the specific opportunity you see in your market. This gives your agency a more client-centric and differentiated offering, which enables you to be recognized as the leader in your chosen space.

Developing your competitive advantage

If you've spent years searching for 'uniqueness', perhaps all this sounds idealistic. But in fact, creating a Market of One is based on well-established thinking – albeit thinking that agencies rarely apply.

In his 1980 book, *Competitive Strategy*, revered author and Harvard Business School professor Michael Porter described how companies can differentiate themselves on what their customers value, or by choosing to focus on selected market segments.

Creating a Market of One combines these ideas and then extends them by defining 'segment' in broader terms than traditional vertical sectors.

Another valuable reference point is the 'resource-based view' (RBV) of company attributes, as popularized by Jay Barney's 1991 article, *Firm Resources and Sustained Competitive Advantage*. This is about utilizing the capabilities, competencies and assets most likely to deliver a competitive advantage, as per the so-called 'VRIN' model:

- **Valuable**: Solving specific problems
- **Rare**: Bringing unique perspectives and experience
- **Inimitable**: Building on authentic beliefs
- **Non-substitutable**: Delivering outcomes that others can't.

By combining highly focused differentiation, a discrete target audience and the application of your unique qualities, you can create a Market of One.

Ultimately, you're cultivating ownability – like Coca-Cola owns 'happiness' or Kit-Kat owns the idea of 'having a break'. But as well as simple distinctiveness and consistency, building a unique and tangible offer also adds deeper relevance for your chosen audience.

I should also add that *unlike* Coke and Kit-Kat, you're doing all this without relying on vast marketing budgets (you'll find out how in Chapter 8).

To create and sustain this kind of competitive advantage, you'll need to reject traditional agency habits around positioning, culture, sales and pricing, and then adopt more intentional, modern and effective behaviours. That's what this book is about.

Whether you want to accelerate from good to great, or turn around poor performance, to develop, implement and sustain your Market of One is an empowering act of commercial transformation.

Create a virtuous circle

You'll know you're thriving in your Market of One when you consistently achieve the results that you want, you regularly outperform your competitors, and your points of difference are impossible for other agencies to copy.

Here are the characteristics to cultivate:

- **Client impact:** When you describe what you offer, clients lean in. Instead of radio silence after credentials meetings, your offer informs their agenda and uncovers immediate opportunities. And once you're delivering results, it's far harder for other agencies to find an opening.

- **New-business**: You have more leads, win more often and convert opportunities faster. And because clients need what you have, they treat you like an expert and demand your best work.

- **Profit**: You charge what you're worth and operate more efficiently. By leveraging your uniqueness, you can price in a way that avoids over-servicing and delivers healthy margins.

- **Talent**: Great people are easier to find and retain. You become a beacon for the best talent in the market, and you have the resources to reward them well and protect them from burnout. And if they work for you, they're not working for your competitors.

- **Clarity**: Everyone knows who you are and what you stand for. That includes you, your leadership team, your people, your clients and your prospects, not to mention the trade press and other industry stakeholders.

- **Alignment**: Your leadership team is on the same page. Instead of endless discussions about what to do, your board meetings are focused on real progress towards agreed outcomes. Likewise, your team know their roles and operate with shared values.

- **Confidence**: As an organization, you're aware of the value of your expertise. Your people feel empowered to lead their client conversations and fearlessly offer their informed advice.

- **Work**: With top talent, a strong culture and trusted client relationships, you can focus more on your work, and approach it with greater clarity and belief.

Wherever you're at, know that everything you see here is within reach. Being in a Market of One creates a virtuous circle where each of these benefits supports the others

– especially happy people doing better work, which creates more satisfied clients.

To understand to what degree you're already achieving these aims, you can complete Co:definery's Diagnostic Questionnaire at www.codefinery.com/dq

The business case for change

Clearly this virtuous circle will improve your commercial performance. But 'by how much?', I hear you ask. And 'is the investment worth it?', I hear you think (yes, I hear thoughts too).

To illustrate your potential gains, new-business performance is a handy proxy for wider commercial success. In an under-differentiated market, many agencies treat finding new clients as a volume game. More is always better – more clients, via more meetings, more proposals and more pitches. Depending on your agency model, that may or may not be working for you, but I'm sure it's exhausting.

Instead of just dialling your effort up to 11, what's less well understood is how transformational it can be to adjust variables other than volume.[1] Here are a few examples:

- Do you really need more meetings, or would you be better off converting more conversations into real opportunities?

- What's the relationship between your pitch volume, pitch costs and annual revenue?

- What has more impact on annual revenue – average deal size or the number of pitches you contest?

---

[1] If you haven't watched the movie *This is Spinal Tap*, then you really should.

By understanding these inter-related dynamics, you soon recognize that volume might not be the ideal path to growth. More specifically, once your ideal clients see you as tangibly different, you have far greater influence on conversion as you progress down your sales funnel. You generate bigger numbers – and better clients – with less wasted energy, money and morale.

This is what being in Market of One can do. Meaningful difference drives sales success. You'll read more about that in Chapter 9.

In the meantime, you can explore how these dynamics impact your own agency by using Co:definery's Business Case Calculator. Plug in your own numbers and see how each tweak impacts your commercial performance. Just head to www.codefinery.com/bcc

Benefits beyond new-business

Clearly deep differentiation has a dramatic impact on new-business, with some very healthy consequences for your finances. But that's far from the only argument for creating your Market of One. More efficiently winning more right-fit clients offers a range of other benefits. These include:

- **Greater client impact**: Better relationships are the perfect platform for higher quality work and improved client outcomes.
- **Improved organic growth**: Swapping painful loss-leaders for growth-ready relationships is a gift to your account people.
- **Reduced new-business pressure**: Improved organic growth also means you need fewer new client wins to hit your overall numbers.
- **Reduced opportunity cost**: Less pressure and more success have a major impact on morale and your

credibility as a leader. Imagine what else you might achieve with all those good vibes.

- **Pitching efficiency**: Getting operationally slicker reduces your internal pitch costs.
- **Reputational improvement**: From awards to commercial success, there's an uplift in the profile and perception of your agency in the market. As a bonus, you're also creating fear in the minds of your competitors – no-one relishes pitching against the hot shop.
- **Talent attraction and retention**: Yes, I know this was also in the previous list of virtuous circle qualities, but it's worth emphasizing – world-class people demand to win, so you're making it easy for them to join, stay and thrive.
- **Profit to reinvest**: From perks and training, to creating a more diverse, equitable and inclusive culture, more cash helps you build a better agency.

With all this in mind, the case for creating a Market of One should be clear. The question isn't whether you can afford to change, it's whether you can afford not to.

Liberation beckons

The aim of Chapter 1 has been to demonstrate the perils of the Oversupply Myth and introduce a Market of One as your escape route. The ultimate goal is for you to consistently feel focused, invigorated and fulfilled, which will also profoundly impact the people around you. Changing direction could be the most rewarding decision of your career.

But while there's unlimited upside, you also have plenty of work to do. Your liberation starts with a reality check. Be warned – there are difficult truths ahead. It's time to remove your blinkers and see the agency landscape with a refreshed perspective.

Let's go to work.

Chapter 2:
The Big Grind

To embrace your opportunity to create a Market of One, you need to understand what you're up against. Breaking through the Oversupply Myth means recognizing how pervasive it's become.

That's why this chapter explores the difficult reality of running an agency, which can feel like you're stuck in a hamster wheel. It's relentless, thankless and often joyless. I call it the 'Big Grind'.

And even if this picture is only partially true for you, let it serve as a warning. Without action, it's a remarkably common fate – and one that often stealthily creeps up on you.

As mentioned, this won't be an easy read. We'll cover the depth of the issues, how things got this bad and the long-term consequences of failing to change.

Many of the challenges described here will hit home. That might feel daunting, but it should also feel reassuring. Both of these reactions are valuable. The reassurance tells you that you're not alone and feeling daunted highlights the case for change.

PART ONE: Adapt or die

Symptoms of oversupply

Agencies typically approach Co:definery with one or more of the following problems. Of course there are nuances and the specific symptoms vary, but they're pretty consistent.

1. Straight in at number one in the pop chart of pain is that **top-line growth** is just too slow. Regardless of your agency's size, lead generation is a slog, pitching is a lottery and account growth is a struggle.

2. Next up is **profit**. Agencies just aren't making enough money. If you're regularly negotiating your fees with skilled procurement people, you feel like you have nowhere to go but down. And in an increasingly project-led market, treating initial wins as loss-leaders often anchors your pricing too low. At the same time, the twin spectres of giving ideas away in pitches and over-servicing clients are exhibits A and B in the case against margin retention.

3. Top-line and bottom-line ill health naturally lead to problem number three – the struggle to **attract and retain the best talent**. Because you're running dangerously lean, your smartest people – often including you – have become bottlenecks at risk of burnout, or at least perennial flight risks. This isn't conducive to creativity, joy and client continuity. And your bloodshot eyes aren't a good look when you interview candidates for open roles.

Unsurprisingly, these overlapping issues exacerbate one another. Far from a virtuous circle, agencies are stuck in a vicious cycle. Without money, you can't attract the best people. Without great people, you can't do great work. And without high-quality work, you can't make decent money.

This dynamic sustains frustration, exhaustion and a long-term lack of fulfilment. So to begin the process of changing that, let's figure out how on earth it all happened.

How did we get here?

As is often said, to understand the present you must understand the past. There are lessons to be learned from agencies' slide from respected, trusted advisors into the Big Grind.

Beyond the summary that follows, if you want more detail on this subject – and heaven knows why you wouldn't – I urge you to read Michael Farmer's book, *Madison Avenue Manslaughter*. It includes a forensic account of how agencies' downward spiral tracks to the digitization of media and associated changes in what clients need. TL;DR – everything changed, agencies didn't keep up and now life sucks.

And by the way, if you're thinking this won't apply to you because you're not a Madison Avenue behemoth, then think again. Many of the behavioural and cultural norms of the big shops are just as prevalent in smaller independents. So regardless of your agency's size, discipline or ownership model, you still need to appreciate where your headwinds come from.

A brief history of time and materials

Back in the day, starting with what we've tiresomely come to call the '*Mad Men*' era of the 1960s, life was good for agencies (for now, we'll sidestep the less savoury societal norms that this AMC show reminded us we're still trying to change).

Agencies were trusted advisors to the CEO, so credibility was plentiful. At the same time, the finances were plump and healthy. The media commission model meant agencies earned 15% of the client's media budget to buy the space *and* create the work. And because 15% of a really big number is still a pretty big number, there was plenty of cash swilling around to throw at thorny briefs or dissatisfied clients. Ideas were scrawled on napkins and agencies could keep creating until the job was done.

PART ONE: Adapt or die

From the middle of the 1980s onwards, market forces began to disrupt adland. Publicly owned holding companies began aggressively acquiring agencies and making them less bloated. This reshaping of headcounts was also a natural consequence of the media commission system ending. Creative agencies now had to earn their own keep. This meant charging for ideas, as opposed to giving them away as part of a media buy.

Cue another pivotal crossroads in the evolution of agencies. Not only did the admin-heavy model of selling time become the accepted norm, it was also poorly embedded – not just practically, but also culturally.

Once the 2000s arrived, the media landscape had exploded. The simple world of TV, radio, print and outdoor was no more, replaced by an inconceivable increase in the volume of deliverables. Agency workloads went ballistic, which would've been good news had there been a more reliable way of converting demand into profit.

This deficit of commerciality was exacerbated by the rise of client-side procurement. Having emerged back in the 1970s, they'd taken their time to reach the swollen marketing supply chain. And when they did, they found a weakened agency sector, unable to recognize supplier conditioning or defend itself. Needless to say, hilarity ensued – fees reduced, headcounts dropped and 'sweating assets' became a perceived necessity to stay in the black.

As the years passed, each new round of media innovation brought its own wave of digital specialists. But these web, search, mobile and social media agencies could only briefly trade on their newness before being suckered by the Oversupply Myth. Once each discipline was flooded by an army of copycats, even these digital upstarts rushed to join their more established cousins in the inevitable race to the bottom.

Welcome to now

Cut forward to today and reality has well and truly bitten. The major creative shops have seen profit margins slip from 20%+ to single figures. Money is also harder to come by for media agencies now that commissions have shrunk and reliable fee income remains a challenge. No wonder most holding companies continue to consolidate and cut costs.

At the same time, the 1960s party has proven stubbornly hard to leave. Back then, like free love, credibility and resources were abundant. But now that these are scarce, there's a cultural hangover where any hint of client discontent is still readily doused with goodwill. Unfortunately, there are fewer resources to throw at problems and less credibility with which to smooth-talk your way out of tight spots.

Some examples are obvious, like free amends for grumpy clients. But it's also more insidiously present – witness the common promise that your pitch team will work on the client's business. That's usually stretching the truth – I mean, who keeps their top people idling on the bench? – so inevitably promises get broken and more credibility erodes.

These are just two examples of an ever-present urge to placate omnipotent clients who could discard you at any moment. If you're familiar with 'anxious attachment', you'll know that this fear isn't healthy. That's the Oversupply Myth, right there.

And then of course there's the pricing conundrum. Having half-arsed the adoption of selling time, agencies mostly struggle with valuing, tracking and charging for their hours. To confirm, everyone's cool with free pitches, yeah? And can I get a high-five for timesheets? No, I can't.

Most fundamentally, few agencies have consistently decoupled the value of an idea from the time taken to create it. For an industry built on creativity, that is not a healthy place to be. It's hardly surprising that everyone's so worn down.

PART ONE: Adapt or die

The commoditized agency model

Clearly giving stuff away and working your people to exhaustion isn't sustainable. The reality is that the agency business model isn't just fundamentally broken – it's downright dangerous.

This isn't just a failure to support yourself, it's also a disservice to your clients and, even more importantly, to their brands, who – sidenote – arguably have a greater influence on our populations and our planet than the combined governments of the world.

So it's fair to say the stakes are high.

The smiling curve

To demonstrate just how far agencies are from a sustainable business model, look no further than this version of the classic 'smiling curve'. The original, devised by Stan Shih, founder of IT company Acer, describes how value creation varies during product development. The idea being that value perception is highest at the beginning and the end, hence the 'smile'.

Looking at the following diagram, let's apply this idea to agencies by comparing how client value perception and agency revenue track over the course of a typical campaign or project life cycle.

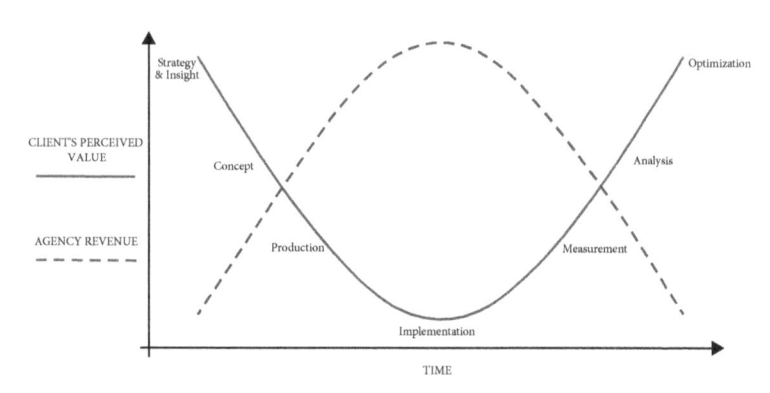

Figure 1: 'Smiling Curve' applied to agencies

The client's perceived value of your work is highest at the outset, when strategy and concepts are developed. It then dips in the middle during implementation, before increasing again for measurement and optimization. Hence the smile-shaped curve.

Sadly, over the same time frame, the agency revenue curve is the exact reverse. You make money on the hard yards in the middle, but struggle to monetize your thinking at the start or your analysis at the end.

In essence, your clients most value what you give away and you make your money from what they value least. Honestly, it would be comical if it wasn't so widespread.

Of course this is a generalized example, so it won't apply to every project type for every agency. But as a high-level illustration of what's perpetuating the Big Grind, the mismatch of value and revenue offers a salutary lesson.

The lack of commerciality

Now you understand the history and beating heart of the Big Grind, you have a sense of why agencies' collective health is as bad as it is. But to appreciate the day-to-day impact of commoditization, we need to dig deeper.

What we find is an absence of commercially minded behaviours. Thankfully, by flagging three common symptoms here, you'll start to see them everywhere. And that will help you make changes.

The leaky bucket

First of all, agencies have a real issue with clients leaving faster than they're replaced. It's the classic 'leaky bucket'. In fact, this metaphor for agency life is so well established that it's passed from cliché to convention. That's seriously bad business.

PART ONE: Adapt or die

In fairness, more clients favouring projects over retainers has made this worse. But there's a deeper cultural issue here – our obsession with winning pitches. Many decades ago, account tenures were long, so client departures were rare. No wonder the exciting new world of new-business became so seductive.

From the brief to the pitch and the prize, everything dazzled with novelty and urgency. Reputations were built and advertising icons were born – from taglines and brand mascots, to the creative legends we still quote to this day. Even the stories of epic pitch fails became the fabric of agency folklore.

At the same time, hidden behind this conveyor belt of iconography, client services quietly went about the business of keeping business. It's not that organic growth wasn't welcome or well-rewarded, but the discipline of account handling was never bestowed with the front-row status of new-business.

After decades of this conditioning, agencies now have a dangerously unbalanced approach to growth. Your investment – and the energy of your best people – consistently flows more towards client acquisition than client success.

Your account people can't win – figuratively or literally. Often lambasted as 'bag carriers', their status as advisors to your client's CEO is now dusty nostalgia. At the same time, they're often handed loss-leader accounts with under-staffed teams, so growth is all but impossible.

Contrast that with glorious new-business, with its big money hires and lofty 'lifeblood of the agency' status. These tacit statements of priority trickle down into agency culture. The message is clear – new-business success equals business success, so your healthy competitive spirit gets misapplied to mean 'win anything from anyone'.

Wrong-fit clients are coaxed in, quickly disappointed and then barely mourned as they reduce spend or shuffle off. In this context, your leaky bucket is more like a drainpipe. If anyone tells you that indiscriminate new-business is good business, tell them to STFU and shut their back door.[1]

Amateur selling

This unbalanced approach to growth isn't your only problem. The more desperate your agency becomes, the more it poisons your sales cycle from start to finish.

Starting with lead generation, such is your lack of standout, the scattershot hit-and-miss approach is pure pain. Jelly is thrown at walls, client inboxes are bombarded and your pipeline is fluffed up with stagnant non-starters.

Similarly, large agencies are unhealthily reliant on search consultants – intermediaries that only exist because of agencies' endless uniformity. Clients hire them to help find the right agencies. And as sophisticated procurement functions increasingly take on that role, it's becoming a less reliable sales channel. That's why search consultants are diversifying beyond 'search and selection'.

When prospect meetings are somehow secured, you slip into broadcast mode – presenting credentials when you should be asking and listening. You hear 'we'll consider you when the time comes' as a positive response, rather than a gentle brush-off.

Your reliance on hope continues into pitching. Weighed down by the knowledge that your agency has no point of difference, you rely on the magic of 'chemistry'. This is risky because rapport can't be faked. Sharing your cyber-stalked 'insight' that the client likes kittens is not the same thing. Likewise, it's transparently self-serving to show up with a rictus grin, gushing forth with servile hot air like 'oh, thank you SO much for this opportunity' and 'we'd LOVE to work on your AMAZING brand'.

---

[1] STFU – if you don't know, just Google it.

Even if you win, being told that your success was down to 'wanting it more' is far from a triumph. In effect, that's the client telling you that the quality they value most is your willingness to 'go the extra mile', which is code for 'answer their emails at 10pm'. That's also why they knew you wouldn't push back when they imposed their 180 day payment terms on you.

Whatever does make it through your drinking straw of a funnel leads us neatly back to account growth. How you expect your much-maligned suits to make lemonade out of new-business won on cost and neediness is anyone's guess.

To one degree or another, this omnishambles is what sales 'culture' looks like in many agencies. The so-called 'new-business machine' works hard, but for what? An industry-standard, one-in-three conversion rate that barely recoups your total investment in any given year? In an increasingly project-driven world, hoping to make your money in year two isn't just risky – it's complacency to the point of negligence.

This lack of realism is evident throughout your sales funnel. When we use Co:definery's Business Case Calculator (see Chapter 1) to assess agency conversion rates from top to bottom, we often find a self-imposed calamity. If your financial target is too high and your average deal size is too low, you need dozens of creds meetings every month just to keep your head above water. That kind of ridiculous run-rate is a demoralizing way to (fail to) earn a living.

Being on top of these numbers is basic stuff. Without them, you're driving blindfolded, heading for a car crash in slow motion. It's a bitter irony that the leaders who blithely describe sales as a 'numbers game' are usually the least commercially minded.

The Partnership Delusion

The third painful symptom of commoditization is a collective mindset I call the 'Partnership Delusion'. It's a shared fever dream that agencies somehow remain genuine partners to their clients. Bloody *Mad Men* has a lot to answer for.

As much as agencies talk about 'partnership', it's become largely aspirational. Genuine partners share the risk. They have each other's back. There's give and take, and they're in it together – whether 'it' is the *good* kind or the *steaming* kind. This is a million miles from the prevailing client–agency dynamic.

Also, all parties understand 'partnership' differently. Procurement people focus on the commercials and marketers typically leap to agencies going 'above and beyond' – also known as 'over-servicing'. But when agencies are honest about what 'partnership' means to them in practice, it's usually just being treated with basic courtesy. That's a recipe for co-dependence, not productive relationships.

This mismatch of expectations shows up everywhere. Ever worked on a pitch over the holidays just because the client said it was essential? Ever done free amends because they looked disappointed when they asked? This is why unethical clients take advantage. And it's far easier for them to abuse their power when you hand them yours too.

The dynamic is akin to Stockholm Syndrome. Rather than looking after yourself, you're sympathizing with your captors' priorities. Your team walks on eggshells, forever nervous of upsetting the client. It's never quite the right time to ask for that referral or to set a date to discuss their wider needs.

By the way, if you're thinking that all this is beyond your control because clients hold all the cards, then you're walking proof of the Partnership Delusion. Just because clients are the ones with the money, that doesn't mean they're in charge. You pay surgeons and airline pilots, but would you tell them what to do? Let's hope not.

Ultimately, the absence of genuine partnership is down to you as a leader. Amateur selling sets the expectation that you're a commodity. Then the Partnership Delusion enshrines that perception as fact. This is not the route back to trusted advisor status.

Urgency for change

Listen, I appreciate that all this is… *a lot*. But I'm afraid we're not done yet. Feel free to take a moment, if that's what you need.

Once you're ready, the following three trends describe how the Big Grind won't get better on its own. While this section isn't exactly a frothy beach-read either, you'll recognize why the time for inaction has passed. This has to be your impetus towards something better.

1. **Disruption from AI**

   Despite the obvious folly of making predictions in a book, AI is hard to ignore. It seems inconceivable that this pervasive confluence of technologies won't have far-reaching consequences for all of us. It's already showing up in our daily lives, offering speedy alternatives and shortcuts to tedious tasks.

   But no, I don't think agencies will be replaced by robots. Just like spreadsheets didn't kill accountancy and electric drills didn't make carpenters redundant. That said, given that we're in an age of faster and cheaper, AI will undoubtedly evolve how our industry is resourced. Jobs will be lost and new jobs will be created.

   AI will also have a big impact on how agencies make money. WPP founder and S4 Capital Executive Chairman Sir Martin Sorrell is well-known for his canny use of language, so when he talks, the industry listens. On the subject of copywriting and visualization – two staples for so many shops – he wryly described AI as a 'double-edged sword for agencies that sell their time.' That's a pretty frank assessment – and possibly the understatement of the year. Let's be very clear here – selling time is about to become obsolete.

Remember that the smiling curve shows agencies making their money not from brain power but from legwork. If that same legwork can be dramatically streamlined by AI, then where is your money going to come from?

Don't think for a second that you can slim down your headcount, embrace AI and charge what you used to charge. Your clients aren't fools. So if they're not already demanding AI-sourced efficiencies from you, be ready for a knock at your door.

Exactly how much of the time that you sell will be automated is anyone's guess. But one thing's for sure, you can no longer dodge difficult conversations like 'how much is an idea worth?' If you don't excel at valuing and selling your *thinking*, then you can't rely on your *doing* to keep the lights on.

To be clear, this isn't a doom-and-gloom message – it's one of optimism. We're entering a new era of human creativity. If machines can do the tedious stuff, then the contrast with your brain power will be more apparent, not least in how you can premiumize your intelligence and ingenuity.

2. **Evolving talent models**
The second urgent trend relates to talent – from unsustainable practices and evolving values to the impact of shortened tenures and new technologies.

As profits have been squeezed, so have agency people. The need to do more for less has created pressure like never before. As an industry, we've reached breaking point. Decency has become a casualty of necessity. I recently heard of an agency's CFO who admitted, 'we bank our under-hiring.'

Just let that sink in for a second. Once grinding people into the ground becomes essential for making money, you know it's time to upgrade your business model.

Of course this isn't how most people want to run their agency. There's a widespread desire to create diverse, equitable and inclusive working environments for everyone. But are agencies still the destination of choice for the smartest people? Or a visible and attractive option for the sharpest brains from less privileged backgrounds? Not even close.

At the same time, values are shifting too. There's now a clear disconnect between what you demand of your people and what they're prepared to offer in return. Gone are the days when you could buy an all-nighter with a free pizza and a taxi home.

Young talent now have their own demands. They want input into decisions. They want lightning-fast career progression. And they sure as hell don't want to be working themselves into an early grave for a fraction of what they could earn in other professions.

This tension is emerging at a time when clients are taking a closer interest in your talent. Author and search consultant David Meikle runs The HTBAG Company. His book, *Tuning Up*, describes the increasing importance of your agency's employer brand. As he puts it:

> 'An agency's track record is in the past, but their talent indicates what they can do in the future. Great talent is a proxy for great work, which is a proxy for value. Show me great talent and I see a reduced risk for brands investing their budget with that agency.'

Or to put it another way, if your agency has a revolving door for talent, potential clients will notice – especially if the people behind your greatest hits have already left the building.

There's also an interesting dynamic evolving around the role of experience in an AI-driven industry. Agencies have a dubious record when it comes to ageism. And a senior salary makes you extra vulnerable when cuts need to be made. But this does beg the question: what delivers value faster, miles on the clock or being an AI-native prompt engineer? If AI enables the speedy application of experience, then teaching old dogs new tricks might be more efficient than expecting young pups to thrive without a career's worth of wisdom.

Many agency leaders have an uneasy relationship with these evolving priorities. This needs to be resolved. Unhappy talent won't hang around and the queue of willing replacements is dwindling fast.

3. **Procurement pressure is growing**
   The third trend relates to agencies' favourite foe – the procurement department. As politicians have known for centuries, nothing galvanizes a population like a common enemy. And while competing agencies will argue the toss about pretty much anything, there's one topic that unites them all – the hard-and-fast 'fact' that every procurement person is a heartless bastard.

   This is, of course, disrespectful nonsense. It serves no other purpose than to distract from the pain of commoditization.

   I'm bemused by how widespread this willingness to demonize procurement remains. If anything, it's gotten worse over the years. Alongside the trade press and high-profile agency leaders who will happily put the boot in, it's increasingly easy to find client-side marketers who openly badmouth their 'colleagues' from procurement.

Look, I get it. There are certainly some rottweiler procurement people out there – all snarling teeth and rabid cost-saving agendas. But let's be fair, there are spiky and committed people on either side of any divide. Let he who is without sin and all that.

Anyway, apart from squeezing you on fees and casting a judgemental glance at the pricey snacks in your meeting rooms, how is procurement actually hampering your commercial performance?

Truth bomb: They're not.

Procurement power isn't the problem, it's a symptom. So don't hate the player, hate the game. They're not causing your poor commercial performance, they're exploiting it. As agencies' willingness to self-commoditize increases, so does procurement's ability to drive a harder bargain. Sorry, but this is on you.

By way of example, incumbent repitches are on the rise. When I started in the industry, a client telling you they were repitching was tantamount to being fired. Once a pitch was formally called, it was typical to decline with dignity. Now not only are more incumbents competing, they're retaining more often too.

Why is this happening? Because your day-to-day clients aren't especially dissatisfied and many of these pitches are being run against their wishes. The so-called 'statutory' repitch, previously limited to the public sector, has now become standard procurement practice in the commercial world.

So without any great desire to switch agencies, it's no surprise to see clients rehiring their incumbents. But at what cost? If the whole exercise is a bluff designed to elicit a price reduction, then at what point does the 'win' become a financial loss?

Being grumpy about all this is as pointless as blaming water for being wet. And don't kid yourself that there's some kind of ethical imbalance here. It's all fair game for procurement. If you had their job, you'd willingly do the same.

Of course, as an industry, we can promote more progressive practice here, such as specialist marketing procurement professionals – as consistently advocated for by the World Federation of Advertisers (do check out Project Spring). Another option is to adjust incentives to better connect purchasing behaviours with broader organizational outcomes. These are worthy debates for a different book.

The long-term risks of inaction

It should now be clear that believing the Oversupply Myth is commercial suicide. It encourages the willing donation of intellectual capital based on the forlorn hope of reciprocity. Your feeling of powerless is the canary in the mine.

So let's cut to the chase here. Whether or not you're already struggling, the current model is unsustainable. Continuing down this path doesn't end well for anyone – for you, your agency or the brands you serve.

There's an oft-quoted line in Hemingway's *The Sun Also Rises* where one character asks another how he went bankrupt. The wise reply is: 'Gradually and then suddenly.' The same is true of the demise of agencies (and the marriages of those who work there).

PART ONE: Adapt or die

At the very highest level, clients need stuff, so you do it and then they pay you. Unfortunately, this equitable arrangement has been slowly eroding for decades. Now *gradually* has become *suddenly*.

Commercially and culturally, agencies are up against it. When growth is elusive, the prevailing mood becomes one of fear not positivity. Job security is a distant memory, while exhaustion and depressed salaries make things worse.

You're now having to do more for less, with fewer people. At the same time, as well as clients bringing certain services in-house, most agencies are facing fewer retainers, shorter client tenures and more frequent repitches. Oh, and there's the atomic bomb of commercial disruption that AI represents.

Unsurprisingly, all these factors combine to hamper the biggest reason that people join agencies in the first place – to do great work. Regardless of your agency discipline, it's hard to think creatively when you're fearful. And when confidence is low, it's easy to assume your clients have no interest in innovation.

Speaking of clients, allowing the worst amongst them to steer your ship and define your profits is the very definition of complicity. As a CEO or founder, to fail to take action is dereliction of duty.

Earlier I described the agency business model as a leaky bucket. If anything, that's too gentle a metaphor. Agencies are sleepwalking into existential risk. This can't be overstated – it's time to change the record, switch the station and flip the script.

Time to act

Here's one last example of the undifferentiated corner that agencies have painted themselves into. As an industry, we've reached peak bullshit.

To pick on advertising agencies, time after time they appoint new CEOs who dust off the usual platitudes about 'creativity' being their 'special sauce'. For a start, this is insipid, insular and unhelpful. Clients aren't buying 'creativity' – they demand it, of course, but they're actually buying solutions to business problems. I mean, who knew?

Worse still, those same CEOs then stand on conference podiums to advocate for their industry as a whole. Bizarrely, they now claim 'creativity' as the *collective* differentiator. It can't be theirs *and* everyone's. Coming from experts in defining difference, this poverty of logic and imagination is unforgivable.

Seriously, enough is enough.

Thankfully, it's always darkest before dawn. So let this chapter serve as a wake-up call. The issues raised need only be the death knell for your dozing competitors. Once you're committed to action, you're primed and ready for something better.

So let's turn the page. It's time to get excited about your future again.

Chapter 3:
Six reframes for modern leaders

To reject the Big Grind, you need to replace self-commoditizing conditioning with something altogether more empowering. That's what this chapter is about. Think of it as a software upgrade.

As an industry, agencies adhere to a *lot* of so-called best practice. Much of it is based on beliefs that are highly questionable, but rarely questioned. Unfortunately, that makes it far from helpful. In fact, most agency 'best practice' might as well have been written by the world's most self-serving and price-sensitive client.

If you don't believe me, talk to agency leaders who grew up outside the industry. Ask how many bemusing commandments they found on the unwritten list of 'how things are done'. It won't be a short list.

To be clear, there's no implied criticism here. We can't fault fish for obliviousness to water. Holding these beliefs is only natural if they're the only ones you've ever known.

What's important is that you recognize how these unchallenged ideas sustain the Oversupply Myth. By setting your compass based on dodgy collective wisdom, you're making it easy for clients to undermine your confidence.

So here are six essential reframes. Each one loosens a buckle on the straitjacket of under-differentiation and moves you closer to a more abundant mindset and a more profitable business.

Reframe 1: Chasing every client doesn't drive growth

> **Unless you recognize that your agency's not right for every client, you'll never achieve your potential.**

If you want to create a Market of One, you have to be more discerning about which clients are right for you, as well as those that aren't.

Culturally, commercially and strategically, winning the wrong client will cost you more than losing the right one. Sure, you might secure the revenue, but at what cost? Working with people you're misaligned with is like pushing water uphill – as thankless as it is unappealing.

Just as importantly, how else could you have invested your precious resources to better serve your people and your agency? And how might your credibility as a leader have been enhanced rather than harmed?

Sadly, the urge to compete beyond your specific skillset is deeply ingrained by the scarcity mindset I mentioned in the introduction. Driven by the constant fear of not winning enough, many agencies are hard-coded to chase anything that moves.

Small agencies often mythologize this as ideal behaviour. They wear 'scrappiness' as a badge of honour. Similarly, large agencies enter massive, multi-month pitch processes because they 'should' rather than because they can win. In either case, despite often valid concerns about protecting jobs, this lack of focus ends up hindering your commercial performance.

Trying to be right for everyone is self-defeating, self-commoditizing madness. It's the kryptonite to your Market of One. And it's a trap that you can fall into at any time – not least because it's so easy to tell yourself that you already say no often enough. Spoiler alert: you don't (more on that in Reframe 5).

For now, here's one simple phrase to etch inside your eyelids.[1] Your ability to consistently believe, express and act on these words is the difference between a life of grind and one of growth and fulfilment.

That phrase is nothing more complicated than 'we're not for everyone'.

Yup, that's it. The hard part is truly believing it.

Say it out loud to try it on for size. Practise in front of the mirror if it helps. Once this sentiment is enshrined in you and your agency, then the sky's the limit. Not being right for every client and every brief is to cherish and nurture your own expertise. By honouring the value you offer, you create a platform for profitable growth.

Reframe 2: Being 'distinctive' won't make you stand out

Settling for superficial distinctiveness is a poor substitute for deep differentiation.

Agencies often assume they can stand out by making a few high-level claims. But that's just surface-level distinctiveness. This reframe recognizes that deep differentiation is a very different beast.

---

[1] Obviously please don't try this at home.

PART ONE: Adapt or die

Think of 'distinctiveness' as a marginal difference. It's usually subtle and needs to be pointed out. Explaining your distinctiveness often demands heavy emphasis on one or two words and leaves clients none the wiser. This superficiality is a shortcut to invisibility and underselling your expertise.

In contrast, deep differentiation is a lasting competitive advantage. It's clear, clients notice it and it can't be recreated by any competitor with a thesaurus. Depth of difference is how smart agencies grow.

Symptoms of Meh

Settling for distinctiveness over differentiation is endemic. That's why agency rhetoric is so similar. Witness wall-to-wall versions of 'we do great work for great brands'. I call these uninspiring attempts to stand out 'Symptoms of Meh'.

If you're unfamiliar with 'meh', just imagine a teenager expressing their withering indifference. Not the response you want from clients.

Here are six of the most common Symptoms of Meh, along with tips on how to spot them.

1. **Selling services not solutions**
   This is the classic, *non-specialized* claim of specialization, such as 'we specialize in these 46 services'. For clients, it's like arriving in a restaurant and being handed a menu of ingredients. So ask yourself – are you being client-centric or hard to buy from?

2. **Category generics**
   These are platitudes masquerading as points of difference, like 'we start with strategy' or – kill me now – 'we're creative'. Ask yourself, could literally any agency say this?

3. **Tame provocations**
   These are tepid perspectives that no sane person could ever disagree with, like 'we believe that brands should serve customers' or 'we believe in ambitious ideas'. Ask yourself, could the opposite ever be true?

4. **Rephrasing your discipline**
   This is the enduring temptation to squeeze out a new definition of something well established. These might include 'we win, grow and keep customers' (like CRM, you mean?) or 'we create culture' (a well-trodden aspiration for advertising). Ask yourself, are you just reinventing the wheel?

5. **Inventing new disciplines**
   The more inventive cousin of symptom four, this involves fruitlessly devising an entirely new kind of agency, like being the 'street culture agency' or the 'human potential agency'. Ask yourself, do you always find yourself explaining what it means?

6. **Hedging your bets**
   Often an output of misaligned committees, this is where you take multiple passes at positioning and end up drowning in word soup. Something like this – deep breath – 'We're a creative marketing agency. Our performance and digital marketing skills span data, media and creative. We help brands with media buying, search, content and social media'. Ask yourself, do you get bored before you've finished saying it?

There are probably more than six, but you get the idea. For now, be honest, how many of them apply to your agency? And here's a bonus 'tell' – if few of your team love delivering your elevator pitch, then you're probably guilty of at least one.

Interestingly, many agency leaders do recognize their lack of standout. When I point it out, there are often nervous grins. This works especially well at scale. Announcing from a conference stage that I'm about to review some real-world agency positioning statements creates a chill in the air. There's a collective buttock clench as everyone in the room silently prays, 'please, not ours'.

This collective inability to embrace difference is yet more evidence of the Oversupply Myth. Despite the awareness of genericism, there's a herd mentality that makes swimming against the tide feel risky. No wonder Symptoms of Meh are so common.

Settling for distinctiveness reveals that you offer very little substance for clients – or your people – to buy into. In a crowded market, this is the epitome of playing small. So if you want your agency to reach its potential, then choose deep differentiation instead.

Reframe 3: To 'specialize' isn't limiting, it's essential

> **To 'specialize' doesn't mean limiting yourself to a single discipline or sector, it just means applying expertise in ways that create value.**

Choosing difference over distinctiveness means changing your relationship with the notion of 'specialization'. Unfortunately, this concept is very much maligned and misunderstood. Most people define 'specialism' in terms of vertical sector or agency discipline. Neither is the whole truth.

Of course there's nothing intrinsically wrong with focusing on a single vertical, be that healthcare, B2B or whatever else. Likewise, sticking to, say, media, creative or influencer marketing as your sole discipline is hardly a demonstrably bad strategy.

The issue arises when these two *examples* of specialization – vertical or discipline – are seen as your *only* means of specialization. In that case, if you're a multi-disciplinary agency working in a range of sectors, to specialize would mean firing half your staff and two-thirds of your clients. That doesn't sound ideal.

This is why to 'specialize' – and its even more pernicious cousin 'niching' – is often seen as too narrow or restrictive, so focusing is dismissed as a strategic option. This makes standing out far harder.

Beware the Blandness Traps

The limited definition of specialization leads to what I call 'Blandness Traps'. They're 'traps' because blandness is the unintended consequence. As for 'blandness', that means you're the water in the sea of sameness.

Blandness Traps fall into two categories, each with two examples:

- **Fear factor:** This is about remaining an undifferentiated generalist:
    - *Absolute rejection* – you dismiss specialization out of hand because you believe it can only mean focusing on a single discipline or vertical sector.
    - *Presumed limitation* – you accept the idea of specialization, but reject it based on the perceived risk of missing out on opportunities.
- **Failure to specialize:** This is where you attempt to focus, but don't succeed:
    - *Losing your nerve* – you dive into a single discipline or sector (or indeed both), but old habits die hard, so you gradually make exceptions and slide back into being a generalist. If you ever say 'we specialize in *three* sectors', then you've probably fallen into this trap.

- *Tentative vulnerability* – you decide to specialize, but don't fully commit. You fail to deepen your knowledge beyond your less focused competitors, leaving yourself at risk of being displaced. If your clients don't value your so-called specialization, then it's worthless.

As you can see, these traps are riddled with more fear than a haunted house. And there's that scarcity mindset again. It's the polar opposite of the conviction you need to own your Market of One.

Apply your expertise

Here's a much more expansive way to think about specialization – it's really just the specific application of expertise. So if you think about it, until you specialize in something, then you don't have a business strategy at all.

There's really no reason to limit yourself to a single sector or discipline unless you want to. This broader view opens up a world of possibility for ownable differentiation. For example, you could specialize in a certain stage of client maturity – a classic example being 'challenger brands', the long-term focus for the global independent agency, VCCP.

In fact, once you specialize in a specific client mindset, problem or use case, your options become almost unlimited. It creates a strong basis for effective differentiation – and that can be narrow and niche, or as broad as it gets.

After all, the holding companies are enormous, but they're highly specialized in serving global advertisers. Likewise, a PR agency working solely in the drinks industry could easily have a global reach. Neither of these routes is inherently limiting.

The irony is that rejecting specialization because it feels limiting is itself a dangerously limiting view. Liberate yourself by thinking bigger.

Armed with this new definition of specialization, you can now reject the false dilemma of generalist jack-of-all-trades vs limiting niche. Your agency is free to apply its expertise to whatever you decide is joyful and commercially viable.

Reframe 4: People don't buy from people

> **While rapport is helpful, it's not what clients buy. They don't need your friendship, they need your expertise.**

Burdened by your agency being one of many, you're probably deeply conditioned to trade on rapport over substance. In new-business, you worship the false god of 'chemistry' because you believe it's the only thing that makes you different. Mindlessly repeating 'people buy from people' only serves to reinforce the problem.

But once you've specialized intelligently, you can enter every client meeting with the confidence that your agency is unique. This makes a dramatic difference to how you're perceived.

The reframe here is that people don't just buy from people – they buy from experts. Sure, it's great if they like you too. But if likability is *all* you've got going for you (and it's absolutely not), then your success rests in the lap of the gods.

Be the surgeon

To illustrate the impact of expertise, consider the contrast between how you'd choose a family doctor and a specialist surgeon.

When in need of non-urgent medical help, you'd probably visit the family doctor closest to your home. Because their skills are broad and widely available, your decision is more about practicality than expertise. The clue's in the name – they're a 'general practitioner'.

In contrast, if you required a surgeon, you'd have a more specific and pressing need. So now you'd search harder, travel further, wait longer and even pay more.

If the family doctor lacked bedside manner, you wouldn't tolerate it for long before switching to another practice. But if the surgeon was similarly spiky, your tolerance would be far higher because your need would be greater and you'd have fewer options.

This is the power of scarce expertise. Like the surgeon, you're there to do a job – to add value to your client's business, not to fluff their ego. So trade on what you can deliver, not just your likeability.

Obviously this isn't a licence for arrogance. And of course rapport remains important, but it's the packaging not the product. You're so much more than forced charm and cringey compliments.

The expertise business

Reframing your personal value demonstrates that agencies are fundamentally expertise businesses. You might argue for the primacy of 'service' or your creative 'product', but neither trump the importance of enabling client outcomes. That's what experts do.

You can happily be a 'do for me' agency that beautifully delivers against well-defined briefs. Likewise, you can be a more advisory 'think for me' agency that shapes your clients' priorities. You can even be both. But neither of these options negates the need to show up as the authority.

Here's an empowering take from Oren Klaff's book, *Pitch Anything*. Rather than treating the client as the prize, remember that they're winning you. There are countless brands out there, but there's only one of you. You're the expert, so therefore you're the prize.

Take a moment to take this in – the client's not the prize, *you are*. You're the scarce resource, not them. That's a massive shift.

Undifferentiated generalists live in fear and trade on chemistry. But once you embed the idea that your expertise is truly valuable, then your confidence soars. Such is the impact of recognizing that you're the prize. You may well have a dazzling wit and sparkling personality, but they're no longer your only aces to play.

Reframe 5: Saying 'no' isn't just about pitch qualification

> Declining a poorly fitting pitch brief is only the start when it comes to demonstrating authority, leadership and healthy boundaries.

To thrive as a confident expert, you need to cultivate authority. A big part of that is what you agree to and what you push back on. Every 'no' demonstrates leadership and healthy boundaries, but an impulsive 'yes' often signals fearful subservience.

To be fair, agencies have made modest progress here. Until recently, the word 'yes' might as well have been tattooed on many leaders' foreheads. But 'saying no to clients' has become the poster child of mild enlightenment.

That said, you're still not saying no often enough, in the right ways, or for the right reasons.

Qualification is only the start

Let's start with the obvious, what's your 'easy no' in new-business? At the very least, many agencies steer clear of problematic sectors. Arms manufacturer? Nope. Tobacco? Pass. Tinpot despot of a fascist regime? Not on your nelly, mate.

Beyond that, you're hopefully getting better at pushing back on briefs, budgets and processes – too vague, too small, too arm's length, etc. Quite right too.

Maybe you use the traditional 'fame, fortune, fun' qualification model. It's better than nothing, but it still allows you to make the case for pretty much anything ('ooh, visiting that bomb factory sounds fun!').

Better still, perhaps you use a bespoke scorecard that reflects your unique expertise and aspirations. If so, congratulations. That's smart practice – and not as prevalent as you might expect.

But here's the thing, empowering as all this is, it's usually limited to the upfront assessment of pitch briefs. And even then, only when they land on your doorstep via a search consultant or inbound enquiry. You should apply the same rigour to homegrown opportunities too.

Maintain healthy boundaries

However you raise the bar for upfront qualification, you'll dodge plenty of hospital passes. That's great, but it's still only the tip of the 'no' iceberg. It's just as essential throughout the pitch process and beyond.

Fearful agencies mistakenly believe that a 'yes' at the start cannot be a 'no' later. Honestly, is there *any* area of life where thinking 'oh well, I've said yes now…' is a decent idea?

For a start it locks you into pitches that you really need to exit. Failing to bail wastes money and morale long after you realize you're not going to win. That's just plain daft.

Also be aware that holding back a 'no' means you're not just riding roughshod over your boundaries, you're giving clients your implicit consent to do the same. If you compromise your principles to secure a pitch, don't be surprised if the client ends up treating you badly – all pulled ranks, bad manners and need-it-by-Mondays.

Servility here ensures servility later, making client growth twice as hard and half as fun. This serves neither party. Greg Hahn is one of the founders of US creative agency Mischief @ No Fixed Address. When he appeared on Co:definery's podcast, he described this behaviour as 'malicious obedience'. Spot-on, Greg.

Guarding healthy boundaries isn't always easy. But it's an essential driver of success. Whether you're pushing back on terms, challenging a brief or simply saying no, you're cultivating your all-important authority as an expert.

I'm guessing you want smart, collaborative and open-minded clients? Standing firm is a great way of unearthing them. Even if expecting 'yes' means the client takes your first 'no' badly, don't be surprised to find them circling back once they realize you were right. Maybe not today, maybe not tomorrow – but when an expert says 'no', it's often the first step to hearing 'yes'.

Speaking truth to power is really just advocating for what you believe in. This practice has a profound long-term impact – on your conscience, as well as your commercials. Saying no graciously, early and often – and for the right reasons – means you always win. You demonstrate strong leadership and protect morale.

Reframe 6: A strapline is not a strategy

A pithy new phrase in your creds deck is not the same as a robust business strategy.

You've probably noticed a recurring theme of superficiality, or more specifically, a fundamental lack of strategic depth.

Your final reframe explains why this is a massive barrier to differentiation.

This problem of style over substance is most evident in the language of standout. When agencies talk about 'repositioning', they're often just playing with words. And they routinely conflate terms like 'positioning', 'proposition' and 'strapline'.

But these terms are the building blocks of competitive advantage. Unless you use them wisely, you won't achieve the desired effect.

All talk, no strategy

A CEO once told me how his agency had been busy working on their new 'proposition' statement for several months. They'd aligned at board level, got buy-in from middle management and were ready to launch.

Unfortunately, they then discovered that another agency was already using the word 'meaningful' – a word that was central to their own line. So they'd frustratedly decided to go back to the start.

The other agency wasn't even a competitor of theirs. But the CEO felt that once this word wasn't ownable, then their entire approach was no longer viable. All those months wasted because of a single superlative.

The insanity of this story is matched only by the mindset being so prevalent. The underlying belief is that to stand out, all you need is a novel sentence. This isn't a strategy – it's barely a makeover.

To check your own strategic rigour, here's an easy test. Imagine you're talking to your bank manager about a business loan. They're intelligent and interested but have no prior knowledge of your agency or how the industry works. Buzzwords and accepted wisdom aren't going to cut it.

To secure the money, you're going to need solid answers to some basic questions like where you see the opportunity, what you're planning to invest in, why your particular agency is well placed to beat the competition, what's in the way and how you'll mitigate any risks.

If you can offer clear, substantiated answers, then you have a business strategy. And all of a sudden, the idea of your 'strategy' living or dying on the strength of one superlative over another becomes ludicrous.

Agencies aren't consumer brands

Another source of superficiality is the assumption that an agency's strapline works the same as a global superbrand's.

Let's use Nike's strapline as an example. Most average Joes and Joannes could do an okay job of articulating what 'Just Do It' means; something about being bold, getting active or strapping on some running shoes and beating your personal best.

Why the universal understanding? Because depending on your age, you might have over 50 years of mainstream cultural awareness to draw from. When you were a kid, maybe your favourite athlete wore Nike or you lusted after a pair of Air Maxes (I know I did). Even though Just Do It only arrived in 1988, the point is that with a lifetime of iconography, Nike no longer need to unpack who they are, they just need to reinforce it.

This is why your agency can't show up with a snappy new strapline and expect to have anything like this level of impact. Case in point, ever find yourself stating your line, then needing to follow up with '... and what we mean by that is...'? Hardly a confident start. And to save you skipping back, yes, that was one of the Symptoms of Meh.

Agencies are not consumer brands. Very few have any real market recognition. I'm not talking about your mum having heard of Saatchi & Saatchi. I'm talking about clients spending almost zero time immersed in the echo chamber of agency hype. Even the most venerated agencies, with decades of visible and iconic work, are barely famous beyond our little bubble.

Let's be honest. Even the biggest and brightest agencies on the planet are B2B brands with tiny audiences and minimal marketing spend. Of course going big at Cannes or investing in long-term thought leadership means you're building your brand. But that doesn't mean a pithy strapline is going to tell your story in the same way that Just Do It tells Nike's.

Step off the Positioning Carousel

To explain why so many agencies fall into word soup superficiality, it's useful to examine how these positionings / propositions / straplines (delete as applicable) are born.

I call this costly cycle of hype and wasted energy the 'Positioning Carousel'. It starts when you decide that a new positioning will surely herald a new era of success. And if your capabilities include brand building, copywriting or hubris, you probably approach the task with a mindset of 'we've got this'.

To get things moving, someone – usually your Strategy Director – writes some provocations. You might also brief your Creative Director to distil these 'big ideas' into pithy headlines. Unfortunately, although they're both smart and motivated, they're rarely B2B specialists and they're certainly not experts in agency positioning. Oh, and they're also super stacked with their day jobs.

These limitations become clear in the initial outputs. Without a meaningful exploration of where you're going, 'vision' rarely extends beyond 'win better clients', 'growth' or 'make more money'. A clear sense of 'why' is also often missing. And if you don't define an ownable target audience, then timidly trying to be all things to all people gets baked in from the start.

At this point, with your 'where', 'why' and 'who' all unexplored, the most promising candidate statements are 'socialized'. That's agency-speak for 'awkwardly shared so the people with the most political clout can exert their influence to choose the option that best suits them'. Refinements are discussed, follow-up meetings are scheduled and the process rolls on, often for months.

Eventually, twin pressures build. Your need for impact reaches fever pitch and the appetite for debate dwindles. So *et voilà*, your undercooked thinking is deemed ready by default. At best, it's a catchy line that rhymes, or at least something pleasingly alliterative (in English, anyway). And your new positioning finally emerges to a weird mix of relief and self-conscious fanfare.

The evidence of likely failure is plain to see. Perhaps surprisingly, Exhibit A is your own cast-iron conviction. If your new positioning was anchored in something solid, that wouldn't be a problem. But because it isn't, your lack of doubt suggests you're overinvested. Like a patient hiring a high-end shrink who charges a king's ransom, the idea of wasting that much cash is terrifying. Little wonder your faith is unshakeable.

Hollow positivity also shows up in the absence of internal dissent. Aside from your team's reluctance to use the new positioning (they do well to hide that from you), you're given suspiciously consistent feedback that it's *definitely* the answer. You're told that 'it's landing well with clients' and even the naysayers have miraculously become advocates. You push thoughts of '*The Emperor's new clothes*' to the back of your mind.[2]

The real moment of truth, as ever, is pitch success. If your fortunes rise with your snazzy new line, it's hailed a success. But if your fortunes decline or stay put, it's condemned as a failure

---

[2] Hans Christian Andersen's folktale about an emperor's subjects pretending to laud his outfit when in fact he's actually naked.

and you're crushingly back to square one – minus a fair chunk of your credibility.

But what are clients actually reacting to? Being too provocative was carefully avoided, so you offered them a statement so benign they'd struggle to disagree. And such is the similarity of agency positioning statements that, after seeing a handful of presentations, clients rarely remember one from another. So is your new 'positioning' *really* the reason for success or failure? What about your team, their confidence or their thinking? And wait, *surely* it's 'all about the work' or your people being your 'biggest differentiator'?

The irony is tragicomic. First, you invest months crafting a pithy slogan that you ordain with godlike powers of converting sceptical prospects into paying believers. Then after a couple of losses, you emphasize its superficiality by ditching it in a heartbeat.

Let's get real. You pitch your positioning as a deeply held belief, but really it's just some cool shit designed to stick in the client's mind. You're living the old joke often credited to Groucho Marx: 'These are my principles, and if you don't like them I have others'. It's a tiring loop of navel-gazing and failure to grow, punctuated by the occasional new leader who's doomed to repeat the whole sorry process.

Build deep foundations

Here endeth your six reframes, from rethinking focus, difference, specialization and expertise, to embracing your authority and the need for strategic depth. With any luck, you're starting to overwrite your conditioning with a more empowering operating system.

To shamelessly extend the software metaphor, the most important 'patch' is that you can't build a lasting competitive advantage on shallow foundations. Snazzy packaging might create interest, but your impact is far greater when it reflects robust differentiation. You need to offer right-fit clients a clear reason to choose you over your competitors.

You're now ready to reject the Big Grind and create your Market of One.

PART TWO:
Five principles for creating your Market of One

Chapter 4: Your recipe for competitive advantage

Part One armed you with a vision of what's possible, the urgency to change and a handy set of updated beliefs. It's now time to really get moving.

Creating your Market of One means developing a differentiating business strategy. This must be based on genuine conviction, on where you're going and what you believe in, as well as what you're good at and the specific opportunity you see in your market.

This kind of focus makes you uniquely compelling for your chosen target audience. As described in Chapter 1, once the challenge they're facing is the one you're the leading expert at solving, then you become the obvious choice. You stand alone as the leader in a category defined by your ideal client's needs.

This is a powerful space to occupy – in your own mind, as well as in your clients'. Once you're seen as the prize, the temptation to give work away recedes. Your win rate and organic growth improve, as does your ability to command a premium.

PART TWO: Five principles for creating your Market of One

This chapter summarizes the essential principles for creating your Market of One, as well as some guidance on how to apply them.

This is not a manual

Sadly, we live in a world of snake oil pitches offering 'guaranteed' fixes to all of life's woes. There's no need for this book to add to that steaming pile. That's why creating your Market of One is more like a recipe than a manual.

Let me explain.

Using an instruction manual means following a sequence that's set in stone. Imagine an IKEA wardrobe. One misstep and sooner or later you'll have to wind back and figure out where you went wrong.

Cooking from a recipe is different. Although you can choose to follow the steps in order, you're also free to innovate, not least by buying different ingredients or using whatever you already have.

Baking in this flexibility is important.[1] Having spent years advising agencies, one of the most important learnings is that there's no need to fix what's not broken.

Few agencies need to tear everything down and start again. There are always existing strengths, from people and culture, to clients, work and profile. Even agencies that make dramatic pivots do so by accentuating the positives.

This is why Co:definery has a golden rule of 'meeting you where you're at'. This mitigates any risk of one-size-fits-all thinking. Every agency is a uniquely nuanced collection of people, so suggesting a rigid route to success isn't helpful.

---

[1] Yes, that recipe pun was intentional.

For these reasons, the recipe for creating your Market of One is laid out in the following five principles. They're broadly chronological, but your own journey will depend on where you start from and what you need. Perhaps your pantry is already well-stocked with a long-term vision. Or maybe your client cupboard is bare, so filling your shelves is priority number one.

Regardless of the specific strengths and priorities that you bring to the (dining) table, these principles are a proven guide to creating a Market of One. Whatever your route, if you commit to nailing each one, you'll create a lasting competitive advantage, which can take your agency wherever you want to go.

Here's an overview of each principle:

1. **Believe in Better**
   This is about possibility. Agencies in a Market of One choose their own path. With complete conviction on the need to be different, they reject conventions and write their own rules. Even in tough times, they're relentlessly positive.

   In short, rather than feeling trapped by market forces, they have total self-belief that they're masters of their own destiny.

2. **Define your Dream**
   This is about direction. Agencies in a Market of One have genuine vision. Rather than defaulting to year-on-year improvement, they define a destination that truly excites them. And they ensure that everyone in the agency can express why it uniquely matters to get there.

   In short, they harness the motivational power of clarity.

3. **Craft your Narrative**
   This is about strategy. Agencies in a Market of One optimize their business to achieve their vision. Instead of being all things to all people, they're decisive about

where they apply their expertise. And by expressing a truly ownable story, their ideal clients see them as meaningfully different.

In short, they have a focused strategy for success.

4. **Walk the Walk**
   This is about commitment. Agencies in a Market of One know that actions speak louder than words. Rather than relying on superficial claims, they commit to embedding their vision, beliefs and expertise throughout their business. Every touchpoint with every stakeholder demonstrates tangible differentiation.

   In short, everything they say and do makes their points of difference real.

5. **Reap the Rewards**
   This is about commanding a premium. Agencies in a Market of One are unerringly commercial. With deep confidence in their own expertise, they earn trust by focusing on client needs, not just client wants. They challenge positively, reshape briefs and uncover new opportunities. By leading the conversation, they charge what they're worth.

   In short, by knowing their value, they drive profitable growth.

Perhaps you're already nailing some of these principles. Maybe you're miles off on all of them. Either way, it's all good. What matters is that, wherever you start from, adopting them is like compound interest – over time, the impact snowballs.

This offers two rich benefits, both of which are essential for sustaining your commercial improvement.

First, you're building protection for the inevitable tough times. The more you believe that things can be better, the more resilient you become. The more robust your strategy, the less likely you are to be knocked off course. The more proof you build, the more your people feel like experts. The less you rely on persuasion, the stronger your client relationships become.

Similarly, adopting these principles also enables you to be the author of your own success. By believing that things can be better, the more likely that future becomes. The stronger your underlying strategy, the greater your competitive advantage. The more provenance you develop, the more evident your differentiation. The more you inspire your clients, the greater the commercial rewards.

Right, that's enough theory. Time to get cracking.

Chapter 5:
Principle 1 – Believe in Better

Master your own destiny.

Henry Ford is widely credited with having said: 'Whether you think you can, or you think you can't – you're right.' Perhaps he was talking about agency transformation? Okay, maybe not. But you can't argue with his point. When it comes to change, belief is essential.

In theory, any agency can create their own Market of One, but in practice there's a critical prerequisite – faith. That's why Principle 1 is to Believe in Better.

But wait, surely *all* agencies believe in a brighter tomorrow? Well, as it happens, they don't.

Hustle is not a strategy

A few years back, I was running a panel of senior agency leaders. One of them was the co-founder of a well-known agency. He stated, in a very matter-of-fact way, that 'all agencies are basically the same'.

This wasn't just a defeatist comment on the challenges of standing out, it was an acceptance that difference was impossible.

If you choose to believe this too, then you're deciding that success is out of your hands. Having a bajillion competitors becomes a tempting get-out clause for any lack of sustained success. And it 'not being your day' makes it easy to brush off every pitch loss.

Accepting your fate is a dangerous game. If you can't author your own story, then why bother having any strategy at all?

Once scoring is down to chance, all you can do is take more shots. For agencies, that means over-servicing, free pitching, not charging for certain roles and so on. It also means pushing your people harder, even if they're already exhausted and demotivated.

And therein lies the real risk. What agencies lovingly call 'hustle' or 'scrappiness' becomes a way of life. Empty pipeline? Push harder. Struggling to win pitches? Push harder. Not growing your clients? Push harder. Need more discretionary effort from your team? Just push them harder… until there's no-one left to push.

Aside from this being a demoralizing approach to growth, as the Big Grind described in Chapter 2, it's also demonstrably ineffective. This is why believing you can shape your own future is so important.

Find your spark

The need for faith means there are really only two kinds of agencies in the world: the brow-beaten and the optimistic. The former have accepted life as it is. The latter believe in a better future. No prizes for guessing which ones create their Market of One.

Happily, being brow-beaten isn't set in stone. If you've fallen into a faithless funk, climbing out can begin with the tiniest spark of belief.

The source of your positivity doesn't matter. For many leaders – of agencies large or small – the Covid-19 pandemic in 2020 birthed a new perspective. Founders began to see 'growth' in more nuanced terms; getting beyond raw numbers like revenue and headcount to include broader criteria like learning, quality time or feeling in control of their destiny. And network agency chiefs also had their moment of clarity. When sudden job losses revealed an unprecedented lack of job security, all that pressure, travel and time away from their kids didn't feel quite so essential any more.

Ultimately, running an agency isn't life or death. And it's supposed to be fun. You get to have big ideas, wear comfy shoes to the office and sometimes change the world. Yes, it's hard work, but it shouldn't be bleak.

For that reason alone, I challenge you to slow down and examine whether you're on a treadmill or a joyful path. And think hard about what actually matters to you. Seek out sources of inspiration and optimism. Try on new mindsets for size. If you have a chunky salary and a comfortable life, then look beyond them. Consider what *really* makes you happy.

If what emerges still looks like agency life – even some dream-like vision of fun and fulfilment – then you have your spark of belief. This is your pilot light.

Inspire from the top down

In time, your spark will ignite agency-wide faith that deep differentiation is possible. But for now, take it slow. At this nascent stage of your journey to a Market of One, you could take your agency in any number of directions, each of which would elicit all manner of responses from your team.

So don't dive into over-staffed workshops or company-wide values exercises. These might feel pleasingly collaborative, but they're often unwieldy ways of confirming that your agency is not a democracy. When it comes to business strategy, you can't please all the people all the time. Early pushback can easily douse your fragile spark.

Instead, start with a small group of trusted lieutenants. Inspire them first and momentum will follow. Change is instigated from the top down, not the bottom up.

It doesn't matter how you rouse your chosen few. Whether it's sending them to Cannes or just sharing a blog post, a podcast, or even – heaven forbid – buying them all a book, the crucial point is the need for stimulus.

One powerful option is to commit your thinking to paper. As is often said, writing has an amazing ability to organize emerging ideas. At this stage, you don't need a polished vision for the future, complete with a reimagined offering and a fancy new strapline. In fact, to bring people with you, it's often more effective to avoid presenting a complete solution. Even just sharing what you'd love to change is an expansive and inclusive place to start.

From a well-argued manifesto, to a simple strawman, or even just a few bullet points, distilling your thoughts and exploring with smart people is a great way to nurture your spark into a flame.

Avoid inertia

As your collective optimism starts to flourish, it will feel fantastic. But although belief is a crucial foundation, remember you still need to build the house.

I once ran a roundtable for a group of seasoned agency founders. As the conversation turned to creating differentiation, one admitted that he'd been trying since the day he launched, 18 years earlier. His candour was met with sympathetic nods. Then another founder leant in, captured the room's attention and said: 'Same here, except I'm at 30 years.' Like a painting that's never quite finished, both were stuck making aimless tweaks that only their mother would notice.

These stories are painful and all too common. For anyone with more than a few years of mainstream agency life, unhelpful habits can be deeply ingrained. In which case, despite your strong commitment, real differentiation will remain elusive. Inertia is a formidable foe. It's why to Believe in Better isn't just a prerequisite for creating your Market of One, it must also be your constant companion.

For example, if you've ever evolved your offer but traction's been slow to build, you'll know that it's tempting to snap back to what you were selling before. Sure, it's not perfect – that's why you changed – but at least you've removed some uncertainty.

That's why your optimism must be unshakeable. Obviously that doesn't mean clinging to a failing strategy. Likewise, it doesn't mean your life will always be easy or that you'll win every pitch. But it's essential not to respond to inevitable disappointments by scurrying back to the drawing board. Avoid the futility of the Positioning Carousel from Chapter 3.

As you'll read in subsequent principles, being in a Market of One means getting super clear on who you are and where you win – and then staying true to your aspirations. Even when things don't go your way, you can remain confident that you're on the right path, safe in the knowledge that what your agency offers is highly prized by your chosen target audience.

Holding these convictions will serve you well, emotionally and commercially – which leads us neatly into Principle 2.

Chapter 6:
Principle 2 – Define your Dream

Harness the motivational power of clarity.

Once you Believe in Better, you can excitedly ask the question: 'What does a better future actually look like?'

A thoughtful answer is extremely powerful – not least because many agencies have no sense of vision at all. They might have a general direction, but their destination remains decidedly vague. This often goes hand-in-hand with a lack of clarity on *why* they've chosen that path.

Running a business in this way is like taking the first train out of the station and hoping it takes you somewhere exciting. Unfortunately, hope isn't much of a strategy.

This immediately creates two significant hurdles to success. The first is practical. Without a destination in mind, you won't know whether you've arrived or how far you've got. The second hurdle is more cultural. Without clarity of purpose, it's much harder to bring people with you.

This is why the second principle for creating your Market of One is all about unearthing your convictions. Or to put it in suitably grand terms, you need to Define your Dream.

This chapter addresses your lack of destination with a clear Vision statement. And your purpose-shaped gap will be filled by a guiding belief – your Point of View.

Leading without vision

A lack of vision usually shows up in two ways. Perhaps one or both apply to your agency. The first is settling for fluffy aspirations. The second is by being overly guided by your finances.

Fluffy aspirations usually take the form of loose ambitions that speak of being the 'best' at this, the 'leading' at that or being recognized for 'world-class' work. While the positivity can be compelling in the short term, the lack of clarity is unhelpful. It's hardly Kennedy's 'We choose to go to the moon in this decade.' No-one knows when to pop the champagne corks. This isn't vision – it's just enthusiasm.

Being unduly driven by financial goals offers the opposite challenge. There's plenty of clarity on what success looks like, but as a source of motivational energy, it's often pretty limited.

Understand your blockers

The reasons for an absence of vision tend to skew along ownership lines. For example, if you're running a network agency within a publicly listed holding company, then you're mainly guided by financial metrics.

For one, 'guided' is the operative term. You have precious little input on what success looks like. Targets are set and your job is to hit them, because – for better or worse – that is what stock markets demand. Whenever I ask a network agency CEO what their 'vision' is, their lack of freedom is palpable. Explicitly or otherwise, 'feeding the machine' is never far from the surface.

Of course most still want to run brilliant businesses who treat their people well, but they're acutely aware of the constraints. Money is the game and to keep their seat at the table, they need to play by the rules. Their lives resemble those of politicians. Most are driven by decency, but the system rarely poses black-and-white questions, so compromise is a way of life. Getting buy-in is more prevalent than visionary decision-making.

For independent agencies, founders and CEOs have more autonomy in which to consider their motivation. Here the lack of vision tends to swing the other way – towards the fluffy aspirations.

There are various reasons for this. All but the largest (often private equity-backed) indies tend to be light on structure and governance. So while they have more freedom for goal-setting than network agencies, there's also less accountability that those goals be specific. Hence the tendency towards being the 'bestest' or the 'great-work-est'.

This skew is understandable – especially if you're a founder with a network agency background. Having escaped the machine, your new-found freedom is intoxicating. Like you've emerged from a bad marriage, you're determined to forge a more gratifying path, where the work matters more than the money.

Consequences of lacking vision

When it comes to network agencies, a long-term lack of vision leads straight to short-termism. At any given time, although there's usually one holding company that's outperforming its peers, the others are largely focused on defensive measures to prop up their share price.

In an AI-driven world, it will be interesting to see how the holding company model evolves, especially with ambitious PE-backed independents scaling fast and snapping at their heels. The rest of the industry is grabbing popcorn and watching with interest.

Speaking of indies, their own unaddressed lack of vision is no less problematic. The most urgent risk is staff retention.

Running your own show is a great motivator. Alongside the freedom, as long as your agency performs well, you tend to get handsomely rewarded. Unfortunately, in the absence of any motivating vision (and smart long-term incentives), your best people will soon realize that most of the money goes to you, not to them. As Ogilvy's Rory Sutherland put it on Co:definery's podcast: 'It's rather like a market where the art dealers are much richer than the artists.' That's a recipe for flight risks.

Another risk for indies without a clear vision is stagnation. A common symptom is that practitioner-led founders get stuck 'on the tools'. As the cliché goes, you're working *in* the business, not *on* the business (albeit sometimes because you want to). This creates what I call 'jobbing' agencies that work pretty hand-to-mouth. You do okay, but rarely much better. The job isn't without stress, nor is fulfilment completely absent. But your agency is unlikely to consistently thrive.

Now, clearly there are some pretty broad generalizations here, but even if they're not quite on the nose for you personally, the takeout is important: to create your Market of One you'll need a motivating vision.

Explore your ideal future

How can your Vision statement extend beyond benign truisms and numerical targets? How can it become a motivating North Star to follow, not just a flag to habitually salute?

The answer is to really interrogate your ideal future. Think deeply about what you want and how that relates to what your agency is all about. Without this specificity, you'll end up with a classic, away-day artefact – an empty statement gathering dust as it becomes steadily less relevant to what you and your people aspire to.

Consider this question from renowned business coach, Dan Sullivan, founder and president of The Strategic Coach Inc. To build a picture of a person's ideal future, he asks them:

> 'If we were having this discussion three years from today, and you were to look back over those three years to today, what has to have happened, both personally and professionally, for you to feel happy about your progress?'

Here's why this is such a powerful enquiry. First of all, it's time bound. It's not just 'what do you want', which is so broad it's almost impossible to answer. So just by adding a time horizon, you have guardrails to think within. It doesn't have to be three years, but that's a helpful window. Any sooner can feel restrictive, like there isn't enough time for you to make change happen. And any longer can feel untethered from the present, creating a sense of 'who knows', which hampers your conviction.

It's also empowering to begin your mental journey from the present day – not just from 'now', but from 'today'. Whereas 'now' can be this instant, it could also be this week, this month or even this year. So 'today' offers you a clear starting line.

The notion of 'what has to have happened' grounds the question in change. And by combining the personal with the professional, you're exploring both indivisible strands of your motivation.

Finally, anchoring the question in an outcome of feeling 'happy' speaks to a fundamental truth that we rarely acknowledge – humans are driven less by tangible goals and more by the feelings that arise from achieving them. That's why many entrepreneurs start by wanting to make their first million, but find that the money doesn't satisfy their deeper needs.

I ask agency leaders the 'Dan Sullivan question' several times a week. It never fails to make them pause, look skywards and buy some thinking time by saying 'that's a good question'. That's why it's a great way to kick-off the conversation about your Vision.

Build a collective view

Step one is to get offsite with your most senior people with the clear expectation of a meaningful conversation about the future of your business.

Remember that your agency's not a democracy. Leaders gotta lead, so keep the group tight. A good cocktail only has a few ingredients, whereas mixing everything from the drinks cabinet will only ever create something beige and unpalatable (trust me – 15-year-old me *knows*).

In this context Dan's question can be tweaked to speak to the collective:

> 'If we were having this meeting three years from today, and we were to look back over those three years to today, what has to have happened, both personally and professionally, for us to feel happy about our progress?'

Of course there is no single 'we' or 'us', so the goal is to build an energizing consensus. Be aware that this isn't straightforward. The discussion must be facilitated with care and compassion. You'll need plenty of psychological safety for people to reveal what would truly make them happy. You also need time and space for everyone to be heard – especially if the loudest and most highly paid voices tend to dominate.

I would say this, but getting some external support can make all the difference. Not least to allow you to focus on participation rather than facilitation, as well as to avoid the superficial conformity of groupthink.

Go deep on destination

As the Dan Sullivan question works its magic, all sorts of source material for your Vision statement will start to emerge. The trick is to listen out for the good stuff.

First of all, ditch the superlatives. Everyone wants their agency to be great, amazing or incredible. Or the best, the greatest or the leading. This is the fluff that obscures clarity.

Second, get specific. You want fame? Great, but how will you know? Maybe by winning some sexy award. If so, which one – not just a Cannes Lion or a Webby – but in which category? Why? And so it goes on.

By the way, it's also totally fine to ditch the grand ambitions and just ply your trade to a standard that makes you happy and pays the bills. As long as it's a conscious and fulfilling decision, you do you.

When it comes to financial goals, drill down again. Hitting some revenue target or random headcount threshold is at least specific and measurable, but that doesn't really inform your journey.

For example, you won't take your agency from one million to ten, or from 100 to 500 million, by doing more of the same. As the old saying goes, what got you here won't get you there. Any significant uplift in scale and financial performance requires a deeper shift in your model. How will your client base change? What about deal size? Will you need new revenue streams? What about your talent strategy? All this and more needs proper consideration.

You don't need to define precisely *how* you're going to reach these goals, but you do need to get specific on *what* you're wishing for. If your letter to Santa isn't clear, you might not get that train set you wanted.

It can also help to apply different lenses to Dan's question. For instance, when considering what you'd like to 'have happened' in three years, imagine what change would look like from different perspectives, like internally or externally. Expand this to different stakeholders too, from clients, investors or talent, to search consultants, trade press or individual departments or seniority levels within your agency.

Stay focused and follow each line of enquiry to the end. By really scrutinizing your aspirations, you'll uncover the deeper truths.

Find reasons for optimism

Defining your ideal future should feel exciting, like surfing a wave of possibility. But it's also where shit needs to get real. If none of it's likely to happen, there's no point getting high on your own stash of ambition.

Far be it from me to rain on your parade, but if you've been running a three-person agency from your garage for the last 12 years, you're unlikely to hit a hundred million in revenue in the next 12 months.

So why is your lovingly crafted ideal future anything more than hope fuelled by caffeine and post-it notes? What makes your goals believable? The answers are found in your strengths and natural advantages. These are your reasons for optimism – and they need to be objective.

Consider what's truly in your favour. Start by zooming out to explore the biggest of big pictures, like global politics and demographic shifts. Delve into how brands, media and consumer behaviour are evolving. Regardless of your current size or growth aspirations, think about how these trends will impact client demand and your ability to deliver.

Also think about what you have that other agencies don't. Go beyond platitudes like 'our people' or 'our clients'. That's not going to cut it. And this isn't the time to be coy either, so call out what you're *really* good at and why this makes for an achievable future.

Be honest about hurdles

Continuing the theme of needing to get real, you also need to capture the hurdles to your ideal future. You can't plot a strategy to reach your destination if you don't know what's in the way.

That's why agreeing your specific blockers is just as important as defining your strengths. If you've seen the movie *Twins*, this task is the unpleasant Danny de Vito to his angelic twin, Arnold Schwarzenegger.

Review each of your emerging goals. You've considered what justifies their inclusion, now go deep about what's yet to be solved. As a leadership team, be forensic – it's time for serious candour. Treat one another with respect, of course, but there's no kindness in dodging the issues.

If your work isn't up to scratch, then call it. If you want to trade on provenance, but can't measure your impact, it's time to say so. If your future revenues rely on consultative client leadership, but your people are order takers, then honestly acknowledge it.

By clarifying what's blocking your ideal future, you take a giant leap towards getting there. These frank, energizing and, at times, confronting conversations are transformational. They produce the richest source material for a meaningful vision. Seriously, this stuff is rocket fuel.

Distil your Vision

Your next task is distillation. An effective Vision statement is clear, practical and relatable. It doesn't just state your destination and the metrics associated with getting there, it also explicitly defines your reasons for optimism and the hurdles you'll need to address.

Let's break this down. You'll recognize the three components from the source material you've been collating. The following three-part format is reassuringly simple:

1. In three years we will achieve [**measurable goal**]
2. By capitalizing on [**reason(s) for optimism**]
3. And addressing [**known hurdle(s)**]

Make sure your biggest, most motivating goal makes it to the top of the pile. As you can see, the word 'goal' is singular. As the saying goes, you can have *anything* you want, but you can't have *everything* you want.

By all means condense related goals and metrics, but being focused really matters. As agency luminary David Ogilvy is widely credited with having said: 'The essence of strategy is sacrifice.' Choosing what *not* to do is as important as deciding what you're aiming for. So if the word 'and' creeps into your measurable goal, that's a red flag – you're almost certainly diluting the overall impact.

When it comes to your reasons for optimism, it's less important to be singular. While you don't want an unwieldy list of strengths and favourable trends, it's okay to recognize the one or two major factors in your favour.

It's also important to ensure that your reasons for optimism flow directly from your measurable goal. A strong Vision statement has a clear thread running through it.

The same logic applies to the final step – the hurdles you need to address. Feel free to condense connected thoughts into one or two significant blockers. And make sure you continue the thread.

To illustrate the need for this continuous thread, here's a Vision statement for a fictional digital product studio where the thread is lacking:

> 'In three years, we'll win AdAge's Innovation Agency of the Year, by capitalizing on growing client demand, and improving our hiring process.'

The statement isn't wrong per se, but it's superficial. In contrast, it's far more impactful to say:

> 'In three years, we'll win AdAge's Innovation Agency of the Year, by capitalizing on growing demand from our existing blue-chip relationships, developing our industry-first partnership with ABC Inc.'s AI platform and upskilling our account team to be highly consultative technology experts.'

This second version offers far more specificity and impact. The clear thread creates a powerfully ownable and motivating Vision statement.

Be directionally correct

As you can see, a strong Vision statement is only possible once you've dug deep for source material and thought hard about how each component fits together. Although this requires some pretty intensive facilitation, at this stage, it might be helpful to know that your statement doesn't have to be perfect.

The precise wording doesn't need to be chiselled into tablets of stone and revered until the end of days. A desired and well-drawn destination serves only as a practical statement of intent, albeit one that directly informs how you'll get there within an agreed time frame.

The concept of being 'directionally correct' can be helpful here. This isn't a frivolous Silicon Valley-ism akin to 'done is better than perfect', it's recognition that the underlying substance is what matters.

At the end of the day, your Vision expresses what you *believe* you want, based on judgement calls about how you *think* things will play out. There's no perfect information or guarantee of success, so clinging to either will only slow you down.

For now, a directionally correct Vision statement is all you need. Frankly, even a half-decent sense of direction places you streets ahead of competitors who have no vision at all.

What do you believe?

With your Vision in place, you have your destination. Now let's turn to why going there really matters. You might think of this emotional driver as your 'purpose' or your 'why', but it's simplest to frame it as a core belief. I call it your 'Point of View'. This is a strong conviction that propels you forwards. It's the reason you do what you do. As an agency CEO once put it to me, 'it's the hill you're willing to die on'.

Simply having a Point of View creates a degree of differentiation. If you want to be different and memorable (for clients and talent), then just show up with a compelling opinion. But within the context of your Market of One, as you'll see in Principle 3, a strong Point of View adds real potency to your offering.

For now, let's start with what you'll need to develop your Point of View:

- **Boldness**: Like a tree silently falling when there's no-one around to hear, if your Point of View is so bland that no-one notices it, then it might as well not exist. You need to 'go big or go home'.

- **Leadership**: Your Point of View represents your whole agency and no-one enjoys feeling misrepresented, so the stakes are high. What if people disagree? What if they don't get it? While these fears are valid, you need to work through them.

- **Conviction:** Given agencies' deep-seated neediness, showing up with a strong Point of View can be scary. If the client disagrees, then what? Your internal voice whispers, 'surely business will suffer?' You'll need to uncover your inner strength.

So, you've got the need to be punchy, the burden of representing everyone in the agency and the risk of offending the market. No pressure, then.

My strong recommendation is to define your Point of View in the same offsite context as your Vision statement – the same senior group, strong facilitation and an agenda of business improvement.

The Podium Test

This is where Co:definery's 'Podium Test' comes in. This exercise helps you safely explore what you believe in, discern which ideas are most impactful and then distil a singular Point of View that you're ready to passionately advocate for.

It works by helping you avoid the generic, like the bland statements you often hear from politicians. These are inoffensive platitudes that are forgotten as soon as they're heard, like 'here at the XYZ party, we believe in education, fair taxation, supporting the vulnerable…' Sorry, I nodded off there for a second.

You've probably heard – and said – the agency equivalents a million times. The likes of 'we believe our work speaks for itself' or 'we believe our people are our biggest differentiator'. Even if they weren't hackneyed, these statements would still be instantly forgettable.

PART TWO: Five principles for creating your Market of One

We believe that...

The Podium Test works by imagining you're heading on stage at a major conference. The audience is made up solely of your ideal clients. They need what your agency does, they have healthy budgets and they're listening.

Your brief in the exercise is simply to write the opening line of your keynote presentation. Sounds easy, right? And I'll make it even easier by giving you the first half of your line. All you need to do is finish the sentence:

'Here at [agency name], we believe that...'

The kicker – and this is where the juiciness comes from – is that you have to excite half the audience and alienate the other.

Yes, I did just say 'alienate'. Obviously I'm not talking about offending anyone. And you don't need to be aggressive, sweary or show up in a four-foot blue wig (unless that happens to be on brand for your agency). You just need to be divisive. The goal is to find a punchy opinion with real substance – one that doesn't rely on shouty packaging, so it's compelling even when whispered.

This is a big moment. Remember that to be in a Market of One, you can't appeal to everyone. Your Point of View requires deep conviction and you need to be 100% okay with some clients disagreeing. In fact, you're counting on it.

Find your truth

Being divisive and worthy of debate is one thing, but there's one more critical criterion to bear in mind – your 'we believe that...' Point of View has to be real. Perhaps that doesn't need to be said, but some leaders are so focused on what's compelling, they forget to make it true.

To be clear, by 'true' I don't mean objective fact. Ultimately, it's still just your opinion. That doesn't mean choosing a belief that's so flimsy a weak breeze would flatten it, but also don't worry that your Point of View needs to survive a robust interrogation from an army of lawyers.

That said, it does need to be robustly true for your agency. There's a world of difference between expressing a profound belief and trotting out a statement you hope will sound impressive. So when you share your Point of View, state it as an absolute with genuine passion. It needs to be viscerally felt. Remember, it's the hill you're willing to die on. If it's not real, then no-one will embrace it, internally or externally.

Unearthing ideas

Apart from starting 'we believe that…', there's no set format for a strong Point of View. So here are some pointers to get the ball rolling.

Maybe there's a myth you'd like to debunk, a little-known truth you're compelled to share, or even just something that pisses you off. You can also speak to long-term trends or criticize conventions that shouldn't persist.

The following 'we believe that…' prompts might help:

- The world has changed because…
- Clients / agencies / our industry can no longer…
- All businesses must now…
- We will never compromise on…
- The biggest problem or villain in our industry is…

Another option is to recall a painful past client relationship where there was zero fit. They hired your agency on a capability level, but your ideological alignment was way off. What did they believe that made you so wrong for each other? A jarring mismatch of worldviews will offer clues to what matters to you.

Wherever these suggestions take you, remember that they're only thought-starters. It's great if the perfect Point of View arrives in a hurry, but that rarely happens. In fact, be wary of early excitement. As with any creative process, you may need to wade through the crap to get to the good stuff.

Speaking of crap, it's important to emphasize that your belief statement isn't selling anything. Any version of 'we believe that we're amazing at XYZ' is a total non-starter. Your Point of View is not your Proposition (more on that in Principle 3).

Here are a few examples:

- We believe that without a strong brand, content becomes landfill
- We believe that brands are no longer built for the long-term
- We believe that consumers crave excitement
- We believe that quality and speed can coexist without breaking the bank
- We believe that analysis is stronger with instinct.

As you can see, some *suggest* a specific skillset, while others are more enigmatic. Either is fine. Your Point of View doesn't need to be completely self-explanatory. Once it appears in context (e.g. creds, website, in neon on your boardroom wall), the intrigue it sparks can be harnessed.

By expressing what you believe, you're attracting the like-minded. That means you're preaching to the converted, even if they don't realize it until your words strike a chord.

On the subject of the like-minded, as the Podium Test generates Point of View candidates, some will stoke fire in the belly for certain people in the room, but land with less energy for others. Don't stress this kind of variation – it's almost inevitable. Everyone present will bring their own viewpoint based on their lived experience, as well as what the world looks like from their corner of the agency. The ensuing discussion always helps.

Validate with care

Reaching a single statement may take some refinement, so it helps to get super practical. Group similar candidates together, then use simple techniques like working in sub-groups, sharing back for further discussion and voting.

Once you think you've nailed it – or perhaps when you have a shortlist of promising candidates – it can help to seek some client validation. But take care – these conversations require plenty of subtlety.

Tip number one is to frame your feedback request gently. Rather than detailing the foundational role that your emerging Point of View will play, you might frame the conversation as guidance for your agency's thought leadership. You'd like to share a candidate thought (or two or three) to see how much they resonate. Although this is still true, it dials down the pressure.

Tip number two is to avoid going in hard. It can be tempting to simply share your ideas cold and ask for feedback. You might reason that this is how a real-world client would hear them for the first time, but remember that this doesn't happen in isolation. For a start, unless you're on stage at a conference and actually starting with 'we believe…', your Point of View is unlikely to be the first thing they hear from you. And even then, there's a prior context, like your agency's reputation and the title of your keynote.

So use your judgement to elicit feedback with care. A cosy one-to-one setting is a good place to start. Be clear on the context and exactly what you need. For example:

- What are you sharing?
- Why are you telling them this?
- What role does this statement play?
- What kind of feedback do you actually need?
- Do you expect them to be excited?
- Do you want their critique?
- And so on.

Explain that these are early ideas and you're seeking honest discussion. Feel free to talk around your belief – lead *to* your Point of View rather than *with* it. And you'll learn more by keeping your questions open – 'what comes up when you hear that?' is better than 'do you agree?'

Treading lightly will ensure a strategic and future-focused conversation about where the industry is heading. Your client will appreciate being invited into your inner circle, feeling good that their opinion matters. There's rich potential to learn about how they see their role, their brand and their evolving requirements. When I have these conversations on an agency's behalf, it sometimes even unearths a new brief.

All this is powerful stuff. With refinement through external feedback, not only will your emerging Point of View be stronger, but you'll also feel more confident about it serving as a foundation for your Market of One.

Conviction counts

Having developed your Point of View and your Vision statement, that brings this chapter to a close. The key takeout is that conviction really matters.

One of the most draining aspects of agency life – or life in general – is figuring out what to do, especially when the stakes are high. But doing the right thing is easy when you know who you are. As you saw in Gut's origin story in Chapter 1, decisions are faster, culture is stronger and momentum is greater.

That's why having a clear Vision statement and a motivating Point of View is so important. You're confidently inviting your team – and your clients – to choose whether to get on your bus or wait for the next one.

Ultimately, you're cultivating your uniqueness. The deeply personal nuances you've uncovered and built on can't be true for anyone else, so they can't be copied. And as you're about to read in Principle 3, this *ownability* is fundamental to your business strategy.

Chapter 7:
Principle 3 – Craft your Narrative

Develop a focused business strategy.

Armed with your Vision statement and Point of View, you can now apply these deeply held convictions to create a robust and differentiating business strategy. This is what will take you into your Market of One.

Principle 3 is 'Craft your Narrative'. The word 'Narrative' is used very intentionally as a synonym for 'strategy'; this emphasizes flexibility of expression. That's important because your elevator pitch is really just your business strategy expressed with a little panache.

Connecting strategy and expression is the antidote to the pressure of fixed phrasing that makes many agency people actively avoid giving their elevator pitch. It also prevents the robotic delivery that precludes you tailoring what you say to the room that you're in.

So what if being asked 'what does your agency do?' or 'what makes you different?' ceased to be a moment of frustration and became your time to shine?

In fact, with a nod to Jacques Séguéla's book, *Don't tell my mother I'm in advertising – she thinks I play the piano in a brothel*, when your mum asks what you do, what if you could explain without her being bemused?

I know, I know, that's a big claim. But stay with me here. Even this becomes possible when you build strategic rigour into the expression of what you do and how you do it.

Where not to start

Your first step is to avoid a common banana skin – listening too carefully to your clients. You won't create much differentiation by building your strategy around what they tell you they want.

Let's not forget another Henry Ford attributed quote: 'If I had asked people what they wanted, they would have said faster horses'. There's a lot of truth in this. It's not that your clients are fools, far from it. They're just not experts in your field.

They'll tell you that your differentiators are your 'great people', your 'creativity' or that you feel 'like part of the team'. It's true, of course. And all very nice. But it's just table stakes.

More to the point, like you, me and everyone else, clients are reliably driven by self-interest. So here's an alternative automotive maxim. If you let a toddler drive your car, don't be surprised if they head for the toy shop. Just like your clients, they know what they like and they don't think much beyond it. Also, in both cases, if you let them steer, you might end up in a ditch.

Of course client views can still be helpful, just be mindful about what you ask. When helping agencies create their Market of One, I often speak with their clients to search for nuance. The learnings are specific to each agency, but here are some rules of thumb that consistently emerge:

- **Clients are too busy to think about agencies**: You already know this, but it's worse than you think. They're moving so fast that they rarely think about you at all.

- **They have a narrow definition of value**: Clients rarely see value in terms beyond speed and low pricing. You should probably take a slightly different view.

- **They demand innovation but struggle to buy it**: Clients often seek more proactivity and then fail to make time to hear fresh ideas. Their memory becomes rather selective when asked how many of your quarterly innovation sessions they've declined.

- **They have no idea how agencies grow**: Clients' only frame of reference for agency growth is the mountain of crap that lands in their inbox every day. At a push, they might cite case studies, award wins or speaking at conferences. Their instincts for agency strategy are as refined as an intern in their second week of shadowing your new-business manager.

The bottom line is that clients are far from the authority on agency growth, so by all means seek their views, but don't let top-line ideas dominate your strategic thinking.

The Narrative Hierarchy

With that important learning in mind, what follows is Co:definery's Narrative Hierarchy model. It's our battle-tested cure for agency superficiality – and it defines how you'll create your Market of One.

The Narrative Hierarchy is a strategic framework for building on the Vision statement and Point of View that you developed in Principle 2. It consists of a series of components – or 'Core Business Decisions' – arranged in a way that makes them easy to understand and express.

PART TWO: Five principles for creating your Market of One

One of the hierarchy's strengths is that it uses very specific language. Each Core Business Decision is clearly defined, as is the role it plays and how it relates to the others. As mentioned in the final reframe in Chapter 3, words like 'Positioning', 'Proposition' and 'Strapline' are no longer used interchangeably.

Each Core Business Decision is a building block of your company strategy. As per the diagram below, let's define each one, explain how the model works and then unpack an example.

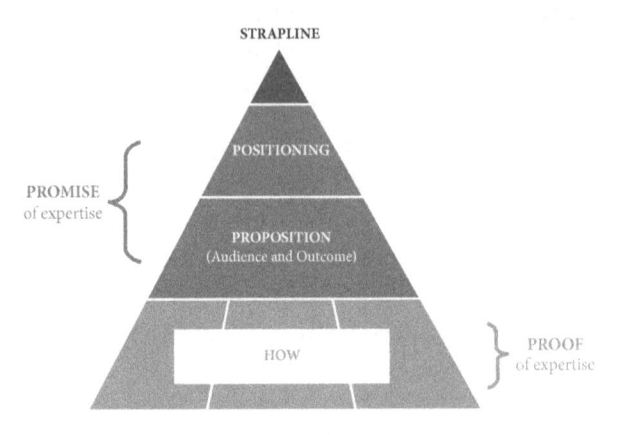

Figure 2: Narrative Hierarchy

Starting from the top, the definitions are:

- **Strapline:** Simply a two-to-four-word summary of your Narrative

- **Positioning**: The business that you're in, i.e. your *core* discipline, like advertising, media, PR and so on

- **Proposition**: The problem your agency solves and for whom, i.e. a specific ownable Outcome for a discrete target Audience.

It's important to note that your Positioning statement no longer does any selling. It serves only as signposting towards your Proposition, which is now a client-centric expression of the value you offer. Together they form your **promise of expertise**.

In writing, in person or wherever you express your Narrative, once you've established a potential fit, your Audience will naturally be curious to know *how* you deliver on your promise. This takes us to your **proof of expertise**:

- **How**: A carefully curated summary of your capabilities, knowledge or processes that substantiates the promise of expertise made by your Positioning and Proposition.

There's a lot happening here, including the breaking of some sacrosanct conventions. So let's explore each Core Business Decision in a little more detail.

Strapline as summary

Recasting your Strapline as a two-to-four-word *summary* of your Narrative is a liberating shift. It no longer carries the impossible burden of telling your whole story on its own. In fact, it's now just a nice-to-have. Although it appears at the top of the hierarchy, it's actually the final piece of the puzzle.

Positioning as signposting

Of all the words that agencies toss around like confetti without ever agreeing what they mean, 'positioning' has to be the boss. This contributes to a shitshow of commercially limiting confusion – not least the Positioning Carousel described in Chapter 3.

Defining Positioning as simply the business that your agency is in immediately creates some much-needed clarity. That said, this new definition is not without nuance.

For a start, let's be very clear about what we mean by 'the business that you're in'. This is your agency's core discipline. For example:

- Creative
- Media
- Social

- PR
- Branding
- Influencer
- Brand experience
- Digital product
- Digital marketing
- Sports & Entertainment
- Innovation
- Content.

The list goes on. I say the list *goes on*, but not infinitely so. And therein lies the nuance.

In recent years, the distinctions between disciplines have blurred dramatically. Ad agencies do social, PR shops offer SEO, branding specialists create content and so on. All but the most cutting-edge agencies now operate in what I call the 'Post-Capability World'. In which case, limiting yourself to a single discipline can feel scary – especially if you still worry that success relies on casting your net as widely as possible.

To get over this hurdle, just treat your Positioning as signposting. It's not there to sell to clients, it's there to orient them.

Your core discipline now serves only as a high-level guide. Even if you also offer other things, saying you're a 'media agency', a 'creative agency' or an 'Amazon Marketplace specialist' lets clients know that they're in the right room.

Proposition as the problem you solve

While your Positioning summarizes what you *are*, your Proposition describes what you *do*. It does that by combining two ownable elements:

- Audience: A discrete group of right-fit clients
- Outcome: A problem you solve or improvement you deliver.

Your Audience and Outcome combine to clearly state that you do *something* for *someone*. This immediately saves you from trying to be all things to all people.

Here are some example Proposition statements:

- Reinvigoration *for* once-great icons
- Accelerated growth *for* challengers
- Populist campaigns *for* mass-market brands.

Even without polished wording, each of these couplets already communicates a clear strategic focus. Also note the following essential qualities:

- The specialization described is far from narrow
- Your Audience may well *not* be a vertical sector
- There's no need to rearticulate your discipline (your Positioning has already communicated that).

Once your Positioning broadly defines what your agency does, your Proposition tells clients whether (or not) you're an expert in resolving the specific problem they face.

In effect, your Proposition is the most succinct distillation of your business strategy and the Market of One that you own.

How as proof

Your How is proof of your expertise. It's a succinct set of 'reasons to believe' that demonstrates why clients can trust your ability to deliver on your Proposition.

The word 'succinct' is worth noting. Your How is where you'll be most tempted to crowbar in all the extra stuff that you lack the confidence to stop saying. In fairness, if all you're used to is an empty Strapline and the absence of a client-centric Proposition, then why wouldn't you feel the need to shoehorn in as much missing substance as possible? This is why your creds deck is too long.

A bloated How often shows up as an exhaustive list of services. Remember that's a classic Symptom of Meh and it really doesn't help clients assess your fit. Not only are 90% of your capabilities common to every agency in your space, but a list is also a particularly thoughtless way of presenting them. At best, the message to clients is 'you figure it out'. At worst, it's 'we don't know how to add value'.

Another common mistake with your How is claiming that your generic process is unique. This usually involves some poor copywriter having to reinvent a series of obvious steps to somehow invent some distinctiveness. Apparently alliteration is the key – like the '5 Ps' or '7 Cs' (they're always Ps or Cs for some reason). Don't get me wrong, a novel approach can be deeply differentiating, but feeble overclaiming is a credibility killer.

In short, your How needs to be a carefully curated summary of the ownable qualities that you bring to the party.

Narrative in action

Having defined each Core Business Decision, let's put them all together as an expression of business strategy. This defines how you'll create your Market of One.

The following example demonstrates how the Narrative Hierarchy works – in particular, how your strategy can be expressed as an elevator pitch. To keep it objective, I'm not using an agency example – real or fictional. In this case, it's a spinal surgeon.

There are also a few subtleties to flag:

- It requires a little creative licence to translate the basic format for each Core Business Decision into a flowing elevator pitch.
- In this example, the order in which the Core Business Decisions are being expressed differs from the order in which they're defined. As you'll read later on, the latter is fixed but the former offers freedom to experiment.

Core Business Decision	Basic format	Example elevator pitch
Positioning	We are a [discipline]	*I'm a spinal surgeon*
Proposition	[Outcome] for [Audience]	*I help elite athletes (Audience) get back to global competition faster (Outcome)*
How	We do that by...	*I do that by combining low impact anaesthetic, innovative keyhole surgery and intensive rehabilitation*
Strapline	Two-to-four-word summary	*Back in Action*

There's an art to knitting your Narrative into an elevator pitch, so let's look at each line in detail:

- **I'm a spinal surgeon**
    - The Positioning is clear and simple – you state your core discipline in a way that's easily recognizable by potential buyers, who are either in the market for your services or they're not.
- **I specialize in helping elite athletes [Audience] get back to global competition faster [Outcome]**
    - Notice the basic Proposition format of doing *something* for *someone*

- - 'Elite athletes' is a discrete, ownable Audience – by definition, it's a smaller market than 'anyone who needs spinal surgery'
  - The chosen Outcome of 'getting back to global competition faster' is similarly ownable – our surgeon can be the demonstrable leader in that field.
- **I do that by combining low impact anaesthetic, innovative keyhole surgery and intensive rehabilitation**
  - Remember that your How offers 'reasons to believe' that you can deliver on your Proposition. And depending on the context, you can bolster it with additional texture
  - In this case, our surgeon might add that 'low impact anaesthetic' speeds up recovery times because it's used at lower doses, which can only be done with highly lean athletes
  - Likewise, 'innovative keyhole surgery' could also accelerate recovery due to fewer stitches and 'intensive rehabilitation' might involve pushing patients harder because elite athletes are accustomed to driving themselves well beyond the limits of the general public.
- **Back in Action**
  - Yup, I went there – that Strapline does indeed use 'Back' as an offensively bad spine pun (don't worry – shit wordplay isn't mandatory, I just like it)
  - Notice how the Strapline doesn't attempt to tell the whole story on its own, but it does work as a summary of what you've just heard.

As you can see, this makes for a pretty compelling elevator pitch. Each Core Business Decision in the Narrative Hierarchy adds more clarity and ownability. The combined output neatly describes our surgeon's business strategy – and how they've created their Market of One.

With this example fresh in your mind, next we'll explore how to apply the Narrative Hierarchy to your agency. As with your Vision statement and Point of View, offsite workshops with your senior team are very much the way to go.

Vision as your guide

Before we work through each Core Business Decision, it's important to emphasize the role of your Vision statement from Principle 2.

Remember that your Vision is your destination. It's a clear statement of your ideal future, including metrics, reasons for optimism and hurdles to address. Here's the Vision statement format again:

1. In three years we will achieve **[measurable goal]**
2. By capitalizing on **[reasons for optimism]**
3. And addressing **[known hurdles]**

Without a clear end goal, you won't know whether you've got there or how much progress you're making. That makes *everything* harder – from daily decisions to long-term course correction.

In the context of Narrative development, use your Vision statement as a touchstone to guide your progress. Whichever Core Business Decision you're working on, keep asking yourself 'will this help us deliver on our Vision statement?' This ensures that your emerging strategy stays focused on your ideal destination.

With that in mind, let's move through each Core Business Decision in turn, starting with your Positioning. As mentioned, note that the order in which you define each Core Business Decision is slightly different to the order they appear in the Narrative Hierarchy (see Figure 2). Specifically, your Strapline comes last rather than first. This is simply because it's a summary, so it makes most sense to leave it until the end.

Nail your Positioning

Positioning: the business that you're in, i.e. your core discipline.

Choosing a single core discipline often makes your Positioning feel like the thorniest Core Business Decision to take, but it's actually pretty simple.

First up, remember that your Positioning is just signposting. Like 'lawyer', 'teacher' or 'surgeon', it isn't there to attract clients, its role is to orient them. So keeping it simple is an act of service. Accept your core discipline for what it is, and trust that the rest of your Narrative will provide ample opportunity to demonstrate how different you are.

But whoa there, you might think – we don't have a *single* core discipline. I hear you, but *all* agencies have a core discipline. Even if you've bolstered your capabilities with an extra *this* or a whizzy new *that*, from a client perspective, clear labelling ensures that you're easy to buy.

In this context, even the world's most multi-disciplinary agencies can have singular positionings – like 'holding company' or 'marketing services group'.

This means that when you're defining your Positioning, whatever your core discipline, there simply aren't that many viable descriptions. Your best bet is to choose what I lovingly call the 'least worst' option. This isn't defeatist, it just acknowledges that no longer treating your Positioning as a silver bullet might feel strange.

Be reassured that you're helping clients navigate complexity and it's your Proposition that will reel in the right ones. And a quick decision here will save months of argument and maybe even a punch-up. You're welcome.

Avoid buzzword bingo

Once you've confirmed your core discipline, the next bullet to dodge is buzzword bingo – adjective edition. This is the urge to embellish your Positioning with all manner of generic filler. These words rarely add much and debating them will take years off your life.

Typically, 'integrated' gets pitted against its cousins, 'full-service' and 'multi-channel'. Some worry that 'integrated' is shorthand for jack-of-all-trades. Others argue 'full-service' only means media-plus-creative. You might also feel naked without hype words like 'creative' or 'strategic'.

Unfortunately, there are no hard-and-fast rules for what does or doesn't add credibility to your Positioning statement. You might insist that it's essential to say that your agency is 'award-winning'. But it depends on what you've won and whether your ideal clients care. And at the end of the day, most agencies can say they've won *something*.

As you've probably gathered, less is usually more. As the saying goes, don't tell me you're a comedian, just make me laugh. If client perceptions of whether you're creative or strategic hinge on you *telling* them rather than *showing* them, then you've got deeper problems than garnishing your Positioning. Neediness is not your friend here.

Even the word 'agency' ties leadership teams up in knots. If that's not doing it for you, you'll need to decide whether you're a studio, firm, business, consultancy, company, collective or even – I swear this actually happened – a 'group of people'.

The nuances offered by all these options vary dramatically around the world – and probably around your boardroom table too. If you're convinced that any one of them makes a telling contribution to business success, then be my guest. Just bear in mind that it's a particularly insular debate. Honestly, save your time, just toss a coin and move on.

Remember, by efficiently signposting clients towards your Proposition without any hype, hedging or hard sell, you're doing them a favour. Don't waste their attention by demanding they wade through ambiguity or hollow superlatives.

Extrapolate your Proposition

> **Proposition: the problem your agency solves and for whom, i.e. a specific ownable Outcome for a discrete target Audience.**

While your Positioning is simply the business you're in, your Proposition describes *what* you do and for *whom*. The basic format is offering *something* for *someone* – you're causing an Outcome or solving a problem for a specific Audience.

That's a boatload of ownability, right there.

While your Positioning was mainly about choosing from a pre-existing shortlist, developing your Proposition requires far more attention. For example, refining down to a single Outcome might feel like an impossible task. And having successfully retired the outdated notion that 'Audience' can only mean 'vertical sector', the task of selecting a single ownable target can also feel intimidatingly broad.

Be reassured that you're not just pulling random ideas out of the sky. Instead, you're extrapolating from what you've done before. That's how a powerful Proposition enables you to do more of what you're great at. It's also why your best clients will welcome seeing you double down on the things they already love you for.

Do more of what you love

Proposition development starts by agreeing a representative list of your favourite client work. These can be current or historic. Note that the word 'favourite' is deliberately subjective. The financially minded might tend towards your largest or most profitable clients. Others might favour the most innovative, the most joyful or the most demonstrably effective. Ensure you capture this breadth of tastes.

By analysing your list, you're looking to uncover ownable ideas for Outcome and Audience. The former is a problem that you're adept at solving or a scenario you're an expert at working in. The latter is a discrete target group that you're highly experienced at helping.

On the subject of Audience, this isn't as granular as a pen portrait or persona. Think of it as a *conceptual target*. For example, you might know the term 'Soccer Mom'. It doesn't just mean mums driving their kids to practice. It's an encapsulation of a certain demographic, so it might include political leanings, media consumption and so on. Indeed, the mom might be a dad and the soccer might be music lessons. The point is that it's clear enough to own and prevalent enough to support your Vision.

With these definitions in mind, start interrogating your favourite work to hone in on where you've been most successful. Your enquiries can range from big-picture trends, down to the highly subjective dissection of each client relationship. Proposition development is very much a creative act.

A good way to break this down is to look at the clients first, and then think about your agency. Here are some client-driven thought-starters:

- Project basics, e.g. work delivered, budget, where the relationship came from
- Client type, e.g. sector, department and job title of whoever hired you
- Client challenge, e.g. their brief, target audience, underlying business problem
- Client context, e.g. market dynamics, competitive threats, maturity, scale, culture
- What was holding their business back? And why were they in that position?
- What were your key stakeholders like as people?
- How sophisticated or knowledgeable were they? What difference did that make?
- How aware were they of their problem? Did you need to educate them?
- How did you need to manage the relationship?

And here are some prompts to help you explore from your agency's perspective:

- How much impact did the work have? How do you know?
- How much joy or satisfaction did the project give your team?
- What made this so rewarding?
- How did it move your agency forward? (e.g. fame, learnings, confidence)
- Why were you particularly successful?
- How did the client feel about you? What did they particularly value?

- How far did your fame travel within the client's wider company? How much did that help or hinder you?

Remember, you're teasing out candidate ideas for your Outcome and Audience. The process is like panning for gold, so be patient. The nuggets are often not in the answers themselves; they're found in the ensuing debate.

This is the genesis of your specialization. So listen hard, follow the energy in the conversation and stay curious. Look under rocks, let good conversations play out and reverse out of dead ends quickly.

Find your flavour

As Audience and Outcome ideas arise, you'll need to collate and discuss them. See how they work in pairs within the 'something for someone' Proposition format. Stay alert for couplets that capture the essence of where you're strongest.

There's also a crucial nuance to look out for. Although Proposition statements are often equally balanced, that's not always the case. Some are more Audience-led and others are weighted towards the Outcome you create or problem you solve. For example:

1. **Balanced:** Product launches *for* digitally native brands
2. **Audience-led:** Advertising *for* time-poor clients
3. **Outcome-led:** Shopify optimization *for* brands

As you can see, the first example has balanced specificity for both Outcome and Audience. With the second example, a very broad Outcome (delivering advertising) can still work, as long as it's for a tightly defined Audience (time-poor clients). Similarly, with the third example, if you have a very specific Outcome (optimizing Shopify sites), having a broad Audience (brands) isn't a problem. Find the flavour that works best for you.

PART TWO: Five principles for creating your Market of One

Essential sense checks

As you're refining your Proposition statement, you'll need to know when you've nailed it. The following sense checks will help:

- As mentioned, keep referring back to your Vision statement. It really is your North Star. For each potential Proposition, ask yourself, 'will this help take us to our ideal future?' Anything less that a 'hell yeah' is a 'no' so you need to keep thinking.

- Also ask whether an abundance of clients with that specific challenge would bring you enough joy and prosperity. If not, why not?

- Similarly, does enough of that kind of demand actually exist? And is it going to continue – and ideally increase – over time? A 'no' to either of these questions means you still have work to do.

Another important factor to bear in mind is language. As mentioned at the start of this chapter, you're baking in flexibility of expression, not writing a fixed script.

Refining your Proposition is about strategic rigour, so relentlessly focus on the *substance* of the words. Be as precise as possible with their meaning, but don't waste time striving for pristine elegance. This will help you make better decisions and save countless hours of needless debate.

Seriously, leave the wordsmithing for later. You might even find that the ensuing clarity renders extra copywriting unnecessary.

Build trust with a powerful How

> **How: a carefully curated summary of your capabilities, knowledge or processes that substantiates your promise of expertise.**

To recap your journey so far, your Positioning orients people so they know they're in the right room. Your Proposition then captures their attention by stating that your agency specializes in solving the very problem that they're facing.

At this point, if there's genuine interest, a client will say 'tell me more', ask 'how do you do that?' or offer some other sign that they're keen. This still applies whether they're reading about you, listening to a podcast or otherwise not in a direct conversation. Whatever the context, once a client is interested, make sure you're able to capitalize.

That's the job of your How. It's a succinct set of reasons to believe that your agency can deliver on your promise of expertise. As you saw in our spinal surgeon's Narrative, it's a powerful opportunity to build trust. The implicit message is 'this is what we do… and we've got you'. If yours is the only agency offering this kind of reassurance, then you're in a far stronger position than your competitors.

Being succinct is essential. As mentioned earlier, don't be tempted to pad out your How with anything and everything that might play some marginal role in proving your value. As Mark Twain supposedly said: 'I didn't have time to write a short letter, so I wrote a long one instead'. Not only is brevity an act of kindness, it also further emphasizes your expertise.

Explore your raw materials

Developing your How is best achieved by gathering all your source material and then trying different approaches to craft the optimum expression of proof.

To get things moving, capture and categorize everything that might possibly feature in your How. This includes capabilities, departments, divisions, products, ways of working and anything else you might think of. Most agencies have way more than they need here, with capabilities usually being the main culprit.

Step two is to highlight everything that a client might actually pay for, and then remove anything that's too granular or generic to be meaningful. This step is highly instructive – it also varies by agency. For an ad agency to include 'copywriting' as part of its How is probably not useful, but for a content agency, it might be an important service line.

These early explorations are all about filtering what's most compelling in your specific context. So take your time, debate well and see what comes up.

Pro tip: having three parts to your How is a good rule of thumb. Because human brains value both simplicity *and* patterns, having three elements - aka a tricolon - tends to feel more satisfying, more effective and more complete (see what I did there). Fewer isn't enough and more feels cumbersome.

Capabilities and process

More often than not, some kind of summary of your various capabilities will emerge as a promising How candidate. This raises an important question – do your ideal clients buy one capability at a time or do they buy them in sequence, i.e. as an end-to-end process?

Author and consultant David C. Baker has a neat way of navigating this. In his book, *The Business of Expertise*, he describes your agency having doors and rooms. Each room could have its own front door, i.e. each capability can be bought as a standalone service. Or your agency might only have a single front door, so clients enter there and progress through each capability's 'room' until their overall Outcome is achieved.

Here's how those two options might be written. As with our surgeon's Narrative, note the use of a little creative licence to knit them together.

- **Capability-led How**: Often we solve [task one], some clients use us to address [task two] and others engage us on [task three].

- **Process-led How:** First we address [task one], next we move on to [task two] and finally we address [task three].

By way of example, our spinal surgeon used the second approach. Their Proposition was to 'help elite athletes get back to global competition faster' and their How was: 'By combining low impact anaesthetic, innovative keyhole surgery and intensive rehabilitation.'

Some agencies like to offer clients both options, so they blend the process-led and capability-led approach:

- **Capability- and process-led How**: We often begin by solving [task one]. Some clients need us to start with [task two] or [task three]. Others engage us to handle all three.

As a big fan of conviction, I don't love seeing agencies hedge in this way. But depending on your expertise and your market, it can be a pragmatic choice.

Truth-based Hows

Another route for your How is to demonstrate deep learnings gleaned from specialization in your field (aka your Market of One). Think of these snippets of expertise as your 'truths.'

To uncover your truths, consider the reasons *why* you work in the way that you do. These 'reasons' are actually highly valuable learnings. As well as being a natural consequence of your depth of experience, they're also a readymade source of provenance.

They might be things you *always* do, *never* do, always *remember*, etc. For example, here's how a set of three truths might be written. Once again, note that you can connect them in any way that feels clear:

- **Truth-led How**: To deliver on [Proposition], we've learned over time to always [truth 1], to remember [truth 2] and never [truth 3].

In effect, you're leveraging your expertise just like a doctor would use their bedside manner – to gently reassure and build trust.

Supercharge your proof

Having explored your How through the lenses of capabilities, processes and truths, you can also try something more advanced – combining truths with process.

Although I just used our surgeon's How as an example of the process-led approach, it's actually a combination of truths and process. That's why it's so pleasing – it communicates a lot without feeling unwieldy. Let's unpack this.

Once again, to substantiate their Proposition of 'helping elite athletes get back to global competition faster', our surgeon's How was as follows, with the truths (aka 'learnings') highlighted in bold:

> By combining **low impact** anaesthetic, **innovative keyhole** surgery and **intensive** rehabilitation.

From a purely process perspective, it's hardly revolutionary. Our surgeon – like every other surgeon – starts with anaesthetic, performs the operation and then moves onto rehab. I'm not a doctor but reordering these steps might well be career-limiting.

Despite that, the How works really well because the process acts as a vehicle for the truths, and the truths are grounded by the chronology of the process. It's an elegant partnership.

To emphasize the impact, here's our surgeon's elevator pitch in full. In fact, let's aim it at you. Imagine you're an elite sportsperson with a troublesome back. Sport isn't just your passion, it's also your livelihood and your identity.

Here's what they might say. For extra impact, I've bolstered the How with the additional texture I mentioned earlier. Note the liberal use of the words 'you' and 'your'; this helps highlight the benefits.

> 'We help elite athletes like you to get back to global competition faster – and we do that in three ways.
>
> First, because we only work with highly lean athletes, we can use what we call 'low impact anaesthetic', which shortens your recovery time because it's effective at lower doses.
>
> We've also developed our own keyhole surgery techniques for the kinds of injuries that athletes like you suffer, which minimizes the number of stitches you'll need and, again, accelerates your recovery.
>
> Finally, over the years, we've learned just how much more motivated elite athletes are than regular people, so our rehabilitation will push you as hard as you demand – and maybe a little harder – to get you back on that podium sooner than you thought possible.'

Pretty reassuring, right? Feeling the need to shop around for another world-class spinal surgeon who specializes in elite sportspeople? Not so much.

A word on wording

As you've seen, there's no set format for your How. There are any number of permutations and combinations that might best demonstrate your particular Proposition. It's subtle, subjective and specific to every agency. That's what makes your How such

PART TWO: Five principles for creating your Market of One

an important part of the ownability that defines your Market of One.

As with your Proposition, focus on the substance and logical structure rather than perfect wording. At the same time, ensure that your language is clear and relentlessly benefit-led. There's no point exciting people with a client-centric Proposition, only for your How to be all about you.

By combining a powerful Proposition with a How that really brings it to life, you'll be amazed at the response you get. Rather than clients seeing you as just another capable agency, they'll be reassured to have your specialist expertise at their disposal.

More specifically, if they're wrestling with the problem you uniquely solve *and* you're easy to trust, then you're very much in pole position – not just to win, but also to develop a strong relationship from your first meeting onwards. And as you'll read in Principle 5, that trusted relationship is a formidable asset in capitalizing on your differentiation.

Strapline as summary

> **Strapline: a two-to-four-word summary of your Narrative.**

This takes us to the final Core Business Decision – your Strapline. Hopefully the Nike comparison in Chapter 3 made it clear that your Strapline is *not* your Proposition. You now know that it's just a simple summary of your Narrative.

So despite perching on top of the Narrative Hierarchy, it's the last Core Business Decision you need to resolve. And that's where we are now.

Treat your Strapline like so-called 'pitch theatre' – that's where you might deploy some left field thinking to dramatize an idea in your presentation. Whenever someone says 'let's do some pitch theatre!' and forces the process, the result will be toe-curlingly awful. But if a clever thought emerges organically, it might well have the desired effect. And so it is with Straplines – trying too hard is a one-way ticket to cringeville.

Helpfully, agency people often have an eye for a headline. So by this final step in the Narrative Hierarchy, a few decent strapline options have usually cropped up. Which is just as well for Co:definery's clients if my 'Back in Action' effort is anything to go by.

If one of your ideas neatly encapsulates your Narrative, then happy days. A good test is to imagine your Strapline writ large on your boardroom wall. How would you feel if your biggest client asked about its backstory? If your answer is 'excited', then you're in good shape. If not, then there's more work to be done.

And if you don't have a good Strapline, don't stress it. Some bright spark in your agency will probably come up with something before long. And if you end up without one, after a while you won't even miss it. Your email signature will survive, I promise.

Find your format

We've now worked through the entire Narrative Hierarchy. It's time to create your own crisp and impactful elevator pitch. Remember that the order you *express* your Core Business Decisions may well not be the order in which you *define* them, so it's essential to decide which order works best for you.

You can do this by trying out different elevator pitch formats. This also serves as a valuable stress test. Each format brings different Core Business Decisions to the fore, which really helps tease out improvements. When I take agencies through this, they're often surprised by how much additional nuance emerges.

PART TWO: Five principles for creating your Market of One

Harness tension

Before we start, a quick plot twist – the return of your Point of View as another component to throw into the mix.

Remember that your Point of View isn't part of the Narrative Hierarchy. Alongside your Vision statement, its primary role is to infuse Narrative development with conviction and ownability, which can be achieved without it necessarily being made explicit.

That said, a strong Point of View can also act as a valuable springboard for your Proposition. When the former expresses a tension that the latter then resolves, it can really demonstrate your conviction.

By way of example, let's return to our spinal surgeon. Imagine their Point of View is:

> 'I believe that sport brings the world together.'

Remember, this isn't an objective fact or universal truth. It's just a strongly held belief. In this case, it explains why a sports-mad medical student chose to dedicate their professional life to their personal passion. Here's how they might integrate this Point of View to tee-up their Proposition:

> 'Because I believe that sport brings the world together [Point of View], that's why I specialize in helping elite athletes [Audience] get back to global competition faster [Outcome].'

Here the structure is *'Because* we believe in ABC, that's *why* we do XYZ.' The flow of Point of View into Proposition adds emotive emphasis. By citing your worldview to justify your work, what you do now feels more like a *calling* than just a simple expression of expertise.

So as you explore which elevator pitch format works best, see whether it feels motivating and energizing to include your Point of View, then make your decision accordingly.

That said, if your Point of View itself lacks excitement, that's a worrying red flag, so be doubly certain that it's as strong as it needs to be. If not, you may need to circle back to the Podium Test in Principle 2.

Exploring options

With your Point of View very much in play alongside your Core Business Decisions, let's get into some elevator pitch formats. There are dozens out there, so here are a couple to get you started.

Translate your Core Business Decisions into each format as best you can, then see what you notice. Before you start, here are some useful tips:

- Say each iteration out loud – insights will arrive more quickly as your brain trips over any remaining wrinkles

- If you've come up with a Strapline, state it ahead of each elevator pitch – this helps you see whether the 'story' suits the 'headline' it would appear with in the wild

- Also state your Positioning after the Strapline, using it as the signposting it's designed to provide – again, this adds more real-world context

- Imagine how your ideal client – and your wider team – would react.

The first elevator pitch format is 'why, how, what'. This is Simon Sinek's 'Golden Circle' from his book *Start With Why*. In the language of the Narrative Hierarchy, this translates to:

1. Why: We believe that [Point of View]
2. How: That's why we [How]

3. What: That's how we [Proposition].

If your Point of View is particularly potent, you might find that this format gives you the impetus to put it front-row centre. Equally, unless your How is pretty pithy, it might feel awkward to delay your Proposition for too long.

Another popular elevator pitch format is 'for only because'. In this case, the spotlight shifts to your target Audience:

1. For [Audience element of your Proposition]

2. Only we can deliver [Outcome element of your Proposition]

3. Because we [How].

This one tends to work best when your Proposition is well-balanced (i.e. both Audience and Outcome have some specificity) or your Audience is highly specialized.

If you like this format but your Audience is too broad, one creative option is to combine your Audience with your Point of View. In which case, 'for' effectively becomes 'For clients that believe [Point of View]'. If that flows nicely, it's a neat way of seeking out clients that share your worldview.

The value of flexibility

As you'll have gathered, exploring different elevator pitch formats isn't about choosing one over another. It's about finessing your Core Business Decisions and discerning the most effective expression of what your agency is all about.

The different formats are really just prompts, so feel free to play around and reorder them. For example, if 'why, how, what' isn't working, then perhaps 'why, what, how' will hit the spot.

This resurfaces the crucial point about retaining flexibility rather than aiming for a fixed and final form of words. Of course you might ultimately choose to imbue your emerging elevator pitch with your agency's tone of voice. And in certain places, your Narrative will need to be relatively fixed – your website, for example. But none of this detracts from the value of being able to tailor your expression for different contexts.

This flexibility is most valuable when there's time and space to go beyond the few sentences in your elevator pitch, just as we did when expanding our spinal surgeon's How. You can deftly tailor your story for different audiences without compromising your Core Business Decisions and undermining your Market of One.

Obviously be mindful of going too far off-piste. You might be familiar with the concept of '30–5–30'. It helps political candidates remember that whether their stump speech lasts 30 seconds, five minutes or 30 minutes, it still needs to consistently hit the same beats. The same is true of your Narrative. Whether you have a short elevator ride or a captive Audience for a conference keynote, the story remains the same – the only variable is depth.

Another benefit of flexibility is that it liberates your wider team from the pressure of perfect expression. If you're a natural salesperson, then you might not appreciate just how much this pressure hampers their client conversations. So if they typically defer to you when it's time to give an elevator pitch, then rejoice – your bottleneck days are over.

Just imagine if everyone in your agency relished describing your differentiation in their own way, without diluting its uniqueness. This builds culture and inspires action.

Don't rush for the finishing line

That brings us to the end of Principle 3. Bear in mind that while Narrative development is a strategic process, it's also a subtle and non-linear creative act.

PART TWO: Five principles for creating your Market of One

Think of it like sculpting a bust. You might be happy with the eyes, but once you've perfected the nose, you realize you need to go back. Your emerging Proposition might have your team purring with excitement, until you realize that it doesn't quite reflect your Point of View. Similarly, as you craft your beautiful How, it might reopen the can of worms that is your Positioning.

See these not as backward steps, but as innovation cycles – each one sharpens your thinking and makes your uniqueness more apparent. The work is worth it. And it's why dashing to a flimsy consensus will soon result in failure. Remember the carpenter's motto: measure twice, cut once.

Having said all this, you also can't afford for Narrative development to drag on forever. One key lever is which voices you involve. While a cast of thousands is too many, diversity of perspectives really helps, not just to enrich the discussions, but also to give you the best chance of recognizing good ideas.

Once you're confident that your Narrative is right, you're in an exciting place. Having built on your Vision statement and Point of View from Principle 2, you've now created a series of Core Business Decisions that combine to form an ownable and differentiating business strategy.

By following this strategy, you can create your Market of One and realize your Vision.

Now it's time to bring all your clever thinking to life.

Chapter 8:
Principle 4 – Walk the Walk

Make your differences real.

The first three principles were about finding strategic clarity. Powered by optimism, you now know where you're going, what you believe and how best to summarize your unique expertise. In short, you've defined your Market of One.

So what happens now? Joy, glamour, insane wealth? Not quite yet.

Despite having agreed your Core Business Decisions, unless you fully commit to living and breathing them over time, your Market of One will remain an unproven hypothesis.

That's why Principle 4 is about implementation. But more specifically, it's about your differentiation needing to be consistently evident *throughout* your agency – not just in your brand and messaging, but also in your culture and behaviours.

It's easy to *say* that you're different, but you also have to *show* it. In short, you need to Walk the Walk.

So as well as covering the launch and rollout of your Narrative, we'll also unpack where your differentiation lives and dies over time, and the need for widespread accountability - from you personally, as well as your wider agency.

Depth of difference

To highlight how important it is that your differentiation shows up well beyond just a creds deck and even a reputation for great work, let's start with a true story about a well-known advertising agency.

They'd launched as an independent and nailed it from day one. Before long, they'd sold up for a staggering sum and the accolades and great work continued under holding company ownership.

Years later, I met their former CFO for lunch and we chatted about their obvious desirability to clients as a creative hot shop. For them, new-business had been about as hard as answering the phone.

At an opportune moment over dessert, I raised the question I'd been dying to ask – during those glory years, how much of a premium had the agency been able to charge?

What do you think they said? 5%? 10? 20? More?

Guess again. In fact, it was zero. Despite their stellar reputation and top-line growth, their margins were just as wafer-thin as those of their peers.

The lesson here is not to assume that world-class work delivers world-class profits. Sure, it gets you noticed and helps you win, but that doesn't automatically equate to commercial success. As the author and management consultant Peter Drucker is said to have warned: 'If you can't charge a premium, then you don't have a brand.'

You're far more likely to sustain healthy – or *super* healthy – margins once you're perceived as genuinely different. That's what being in a Market of One is all about. In practical terms, this means looking, feeling and, most importantly, *acting* differently to your competitors.

You can see this in today's 'unicorns' like Gut, Uncommon and Mischief @ No Fixed Address. And looking further back, it was just as true for any other generational hot shop, like Bartle Bogle Hogarty, Naked or Chiat/Day.

Your Agency Customer Experience

To embrace this need to consistently show up as a confident, differentiated agency, consider what Co:definery describes as your 'Agency Customer Experience'. You can tell it's a big deal because I've started each word with a capital letter. I might even add a ™ one day.

Your Agency Customer Experience is the sum total of all the potential touchpoints that anyone – especially clients and talent – could have with your agency.

The previous chapter described your How – think of your Agency Customer Experience as the natural extension. While the former is a succinct statement of proof, the latter is a comprehensive demonstration. As they say, the proof of the pudding is in the eating.

This is the same logic that explains why Customer Experience (CX) has become such a crucial pillar of a brand's marketing and technology investment. Services, markets and media have proliferated in the modern world, so as consumers we've never had more choice – and it's never been easier to switch. No wonder CX has become such a battleground for securing our time and money.

I'm now less bothered by what my bank says in their commercials, but I do care whether their app is easy to use or their customer service is effective. If not, I'll jump ship to their competitors.

PART TWO: Five principles for creating your Market of One

And so it is with your clients. They also recognize the difference between hot air and substance. However and whenever they come into contact with your agency, you need to demonstrate what you claim makes you different.

The impact of a bad experience

To illustrate the importance of your Agency Customer Experience, let's extend the medical analogy from Chapter 3. As you might recall, we highlighted the power of scarce expertise by contrasting how you might choose a general practitioner versus a specialist surgeon.

Having done your research and chosen the most expert surgeon you can find, eventually the day arrives for your initial consultation. All the obvious signs of quality are present: the fancy building, the discreet professionalism of the receptionist, the framed qualifications on the wall. You feel suitably reassured that you're in safe hands.

But then things change. You're shown into the surgeon's office and they leap up to greet you. Grasping your hand, they pepper your first name throughout a jarringly effusive speech about why they're so thrilled that you're considering them for your operation. This is weird. Your sense of calm reassurance is evaporating fast.

It gets worse. The surgeon then goes into eager-to-please overdrive. Without asking about your symptoms or concerns, they launch into a monologue about why you should choose them – their elite scalpel skills, their state-of-the-art facilities, their gourmet coffee machine.

By now you're overwhelmed. But the surgeon continues. If you sign-up today, they can offer you a one-off, never to be repeated 50% discount on your anaesthetic.

You've had enough. The surgeon's self-serving desperation is palpable. And the hard sell has destroyed your trust. So you make your excuses and leave.

Despite the exaggeration, perhaps this rings true. Replace the surgeon's office with an agency setting and you've probably been that overzealous executive, trying painfully hard to make a good first impression. I know I have.

This is why the way you show up is so important. Clients (and talent) need to know they're in good hands. Even if your skills are beyond question, how they *feel* about working with you remains an important consideration.

New opportunities for provenance

Clearly delivering a poor experience is a surefire way of undermining your expertise. So how can you make sure your Agency Customer Experience is powerfully differentiating?

Obviously your tone, messaging and visual identity must be consistent across all of your channels. But these are really just hygiene factors – just because your luggage matches, it doesn't mean your valuables are safe.

The biggest gains come from transforming your less obvious touchpoints. Here are a few examples. How proactively do you use these opportunities to demonstrate what makes your agency different?

- How you approach credentials meetings
- Your reception area and how clients feel when they're waiting
- The questions you ask new-business prospects
- How you price and negotiate
- Your client onboarding process

- Your employee onboarding process
- How you immerse yourself in your client's business
- How you proactively unlock new budgets
- How you handle changes to statements of work.

This list is far from exhaustive, so perhaps other examples spring to mind. Note them down – they're gold dust.

As you can see, these touchpoints are nuanced; they reflect culture, skills and behaviours. They certainly require more thought than whether your website messaging matches your social headers. That explains why most agencies barely consider them.

This is good news for you. If your competitors default to so-called 'best practice', what that actually means is 'we've never really thought about doing them differently'. But if everyone else is on autopilot, it's far easier for you to stand out.

Products as differentiators

As well as these more nuanced opportunities, you can also make major statements of difference, for example, by building your capabilities into packages or products.

Many books have been written on the subject of 'productizing', so feel free to indulge any extra interest. For now, think of packages as bundles of related deliverables, and products as formalized packages.

In each case, you're not only highlighting what makes your agency different, you're also accentuating how you apply your expertise to solve your client problems. This is valuable proof of your Proposition.

One note of caution. Not all packages and products have the same impact, so create them judiciously. As you mature in your Market of One, you might find that your tightly defined set of packages and products swells into an unwieldy list of tactical add-ons. In which case, you've slipped back into selling ingredients rather than the meal. Stay close to your chosen Audience's needs, sophistication and feedback, and ensure you focus only on what's useful.

Everything is proof

From shifts in behaviour, to how you structure your offer, the takeout from this first part of Principle 4 is that *everything* is proof of *something*. Your Agency Customer Experience is your *everything* and your *something* is your promise of expertise.

Everything you say and do should serve as compelling evidence that your Proposition is true. Of course this proactive intentionality takes effort, but it's essential if you want to be consistently seen – and valued – differently. And as mentioned, if your competitors routinely fail to take this opportunity, then there's an even stronger argument for you to step up.

So with this mission-critical concept established, let's get into the practicalities of implementing your Market of One.

Define your Rollout Masterplan

Armed with the Core Business Decisions in your Narrative, it's time to ensure that all your strategic thinking gets translated into real-world impact. That's easy to say, but even easier to get wrong.

As per Benjamin Franklin's apocryphal quote: 'By failing to prepare, you are preparing to fail.' And failing to properly plan your rollout is definitely a bad idea. You don't want to lose momentum or – even worse – undersell the value of your new-found strategic clarity.

First and foremost, accept that it takes time and energy to embed meaningful change. This is most obvious in multinational agencies. When a new global strategy gets launched, there's often precious little guidance for regional or country-level teams on how to adapt it to their local capabilities, client needs and market dynamics (not to mention languages).

This leads to markets going rogue. The slide with Global's snazzy new line finds itself 'accidentally' left out of local presentations, only to be hurriedly reinserted for international pitches when the top brass will see the deck. Splintered stories emerge, assets are duplicated and confusion ensues – for clients, as well as internally.

And if you run a smaller agency, don't think this doesn't apply to you too. The risks of a botched implementation are just as real, albeit on a lesser scale. We've all felt the frustration of hearing someone shout across the office: 'Does anyone know if version 12 of our creds is the most recent one?' Now is your opportunity to pre-empt that.

Whatever your size, your biggest risk to a successful rollout is letting business-as-usual get in the way. Client deadlines are always an easy excuse for a lack of progress. It used to be a cliché that your agency's most important client was *your agency*. Unfortunately, as workloads spiralled, that wisdom fell out of fashion. Let's bring it back.

Prioritizing impact

Planning your rollout means figuring out how each major function in the agency will contribute to making your Market of One a reality. In each case, this is about prioritizing impact and mitigating risk, as well as identifying actions and owners.

To maximize the sense of shared ownership, it's essential to make this process co-creative, so once again, workshopping is an ideal approach. Also, although your Market of One was defined by a small team of senior decision makers, as you design your rollout, consider widening the discussion to include more department-level leaders. As well as their perspective being helpful, this also creates more advocates who can make sure your strategic clarity doesn't get diluted as it cascades down.

Obviously the specifics of rollout planning vary from agency to agency, not least because every Market of One is different (the clue's in the name). So design your rollout planning workshops with great care. The following pillars are a good place to start:

- **Output**: What does your Market of One mean for the work you deliver? What work should you stop doing? What new outputs should you focus on? How prepared are you for this transition?

- **People**: What does your Market of One mean for your people? What behaviours are now essential? What skills will you need more of? What's the necessary balance of training and recruitment? Might certain roles no longer be needed?

- **Marketing & PR**: How will your Market of One impact how you raise your profile? Is your Tone of Voice or Visual Identity changing? What are your core segments and messages? Who's responsible for media relations? What about your owned channels – from your websites and socials to your reception and meeting rooms? What tools and platforms are not yet in place?

- **Sales**: How will your sales process reflect your Market of One? How will you package and price your expertise? What are your primary sales channels? How will you upgrade the questions you ask – and your confidence to challenge clients? How will you negotiate differently? There's plenty more on this in Principle 5, by the way.

As you can see, rollout planning is a root-and-branch assessment of your entire Agency Customer Experience. If it feels daunting, remember that it's necessary. You'll need to make big calls about how your agency will evolve.

The output of rollout planning is a detailed agreement about what needs to be done, who's doing it and when it will be done by. Be clear about who's in charge, who's involved and who needs to be informed.

When Co:definery guides agencies through the rollout planning phase, we call the output your 'Rollout Masterplan'. It's structured around a bespoke version of these core pillars, with discrete initiatives owned by the appropriate people – whether that's you, us, or usually a combination of the two. This gives you all the support you need and also ensures that your people play an active role, so they continue building their all-important sense of shared ownership.

Measure the gains

An ever-present feature of a strong Rollout Masterplan is clarity on what success looks like. To help with that, here's an important distinction. As I first learned from Keith Hatter, founder of human performance experts PlanetK2, performance and results are not the same thing.

While results are what you get at the end, performance is what you need to do to achieve them. Ask a sprinter about their performance and they just won't talk about their times. Instead they'll share their obsession with staying low out of the blocks or perfecting their dip for the line.

This distinction is easy to forget. In Chapter 2, you read about the laissez-faire attitude that many agencies have around understanding their sales pipelines. By failing to understand their performance at each step of their sales cycle, they don't know what's causing the results they're getting.

The need for nuance is just as important when you consider your wider performance indicators. Of course these will be bespoke to you, but don't limit yourself to simple commercial metrics. Thriving in your Market of One is about far more than just the core numbers.

Well-chosen performance metrics can also help you deepen your differentiation. Depending on your Proposition, showing strength in key areas can serve as additional proof of your expertise. From client tenure and satisfaction to talent retention or operational efficiency, anything that carries weight with your chosen Audience is worth tracking.

To measure the true impact of creating your Market of One, rollout planning is also the perfect time to establish the right baseline performance indicators. Co:definery's Business Case Calculator can help here (see the Resources section at the end of the book). Once your results start to improve, you can track what's driving the uplift and spot potential for further gains.

Launch as a moment of truth

Another essential component of a well-crafted Rollout Masterplan is how you'll launch your Market of One. Whether this heralds a gentle evolution or wholesale change, how you tell the people that matter is crucial.

Here's one learning from experience: don't be tempted to combine your internal and external reveals. Both play different roles. And unsurprisingly, your internal launch should come before the external launch – not least because feedback from the former can inform the latter.

Start with your goals for the internal launch. What do you want your people to know, feel and do? Capture the ideal outcomes you want to prioritize. Overlay an honest view about the current mood in the camp. How is everyone feeling and behaving? What are they thinking about? Ask some trusted lieutenants to help you address your inevitable blind spots.

Remember that this is a profoundly sensitive moment. Unfortunately, change is rarely welcomed, even at the best of

PART TWO: Five principles for creating your Market of One

times. So when you explain the *what, why* and *what next* of your Market of One, everyone will focus on the impact on their own worlds. They'll be wondering about the implications of every word they hear. More or less job security? More or less work? More or less bonus? Am I still leading my team? Am I still being promoted? Am I still needed?

It's no exaggeration to say that your credibility as a leader is on the line. And if you're new in your role or your agency is emerging from a rocky period, then your team's response can make or break your mandate to run the show.

This is why having a robust Rollout Masterplan is so important at launch. You need to anticipate and acknowledge every concern and every question, even just to clarify where details aren't yet finalized. If someone pitches you a curveball, awkward silences must be avoided. Make sure you come prepared.

Another big decision for your internal launch is how big is big enough. Regardless of evolution vs wholesale change, there's no set scale for a launch. While a reinvention usually demands more bang than a refinement, any launch's importance as a teachable moment can't be overstated.

Sadly, taking the entire agency to Honolulu for a week is probably overkill. Equally, a new creds deck and 15 minutes at the end of your next townhall isn't going to excite your team and impact their behaviour. Be very deliberate about where you land on this spectrum of pizazz. It's a rare opportunity to accelerate change.

Next, think about the content. Before you show your new thinking, it often helps to prime people by presenting what a Market of One is and how the Narrative Hierarchy works. This adds context for your new Narrative and lays out the ideal criteria by which to judge it.

Also be mindful about how much backstory to share. To justify change, it may be necessary to include a warts-and-all picture of competitive threats and commercial realities. There are no hard-and-fast rules about keeping your cards close to your chest vs trusting everyone with what might be cold, hard truths. Just remember these can't be unshared, so sound judgement is essential.

The final step in planning your internal launch is where you get practical. When, where and how long? What's the format? Is it just a presentation or will there be space for workshopping? Is everyone there in person? Who speaks and who shouldn't? What assets do you need? How will you get feedback afterwards? Will there be merch: backpacks, t-shirts or yet another bloody tote bag that no-one wants?

This list of considerations could go on and on. It will depend not just on the nature of your announcement, but also your size, culture and geographical spread. Whatever your specific circumstances, if you slow down, think hard and treat this launch as one of the biggest pitches of your life, then you'll be on the right track.

Tell the wider world

Happily, your external launch need not feel so fraught. Internal launch is your dress rehearsal in front of family and friends. The newness is palpable, the audience is personal and the feedback can be brutal. This is where lessons are learned and gaps can be filled. That makes your external launch more like a well-grooved opening night, despite inviting the eyes of the world.

Unsurprisingly, the vagaries of agency scale have even more impact on planning your external launch. If you're completely relaunching a global agency, then perhaps you do need that week in Honolulu after all (feel free to invite me).

Much of the internal launch guidance still applies, so there's no need to restate it. Suffice to say, bringing new audiences into the mix adds nuance. From clients and search consultants

PART TWO: Five principles for creating your Market of One

to journalists and headhunters, treat them all with the same empathy you afforded your own team.

Likewise, when it comes to the practical plans, wherever you're starting from, the scale is likely to be larger. Whatever you're doing, allow more time, budget and resources. It can also help to deploy your agency's core discipline. So, for example, if you have the skills, why not go big with teaser films, social media assets and so on. It will help maximize your external splash as well as the internal buzz.

And one last thing, if all this is bringing you out in a cold sweat, here's a handy tip. Dig up some recent press coverage about agency launches, relaunches and mergers. The quotes are universally bland and the justifications are often nonsensical. When it comes to agencies making major announcements, there's a very low bar, so the only way is up.

You've got this.

Stay on track

Your Rollout Masterplan also needs an explicit approach for staying on track. As mentioned, a big part of this is simply getting clear on what's happening when and who's doing what. But if that was the whole truth, no well-planned initiative would ever falter.

Back in the real world, given the daily pressures of deadlines and office politics, you need an agreed model for governance and reporting. There's no substitute for strong project management, with a regular cadence of sharing progress, celebrating successes and addressing blockers.

If you run a large agency, this will sound like a no-brainer. But if you run a small shop, it might all feel a bit much. Make no mistake, in either case, it still needs to be done. To bring your Market of One to life, you need to stay accountable. Needless to say, an external voice can help hold your feet to the fire.

Happy leader, happy agency

So far we've focused on Narrative implementation from an organizational standpoint. But it's just as important to consider it from your own perspective as a leader. As mentioned way back in the introduction, business change and personal change go hand-in-hand.

Although this isn't a book about leadership, how you lead is a recurring theme – from leading your market to leading the client conversation, and of course, leading your agency. So be aware that in times of change, your team will be especially tuned into you – not just what you say, but also what you're *not* saying, as well as whether they're buying what you're selling.

So if you lack conviction about stepping into your Market of One, then you'll struggle to bring people with you. Similarly, if you're genuinely excited about the prospect of creating a deeply differentiated agency, then your energy will be contagious.

I call this opportunity 'happy leader, happy agency'. The better you feel about yourself, and the more intent you radiate, the more effective you'll be at leading through change.

Put your own oxygen mask on first

To play this pivotal role well, you'll need plenty of energy and clarity. Which means you should strongly consider investing in yourself – be that time, money or both.

Unfortunately, if you're typical of many agency leaders, then that last sentence will already have prompted some objections.

First, you might believe that 'investment in people' is something you *do*, not something you *receive*. It's tempting to decide that your team are more worthy recipients – especially if your learning and development budget is stretched.

Even basic self-care like leaving on time can feel difficult when you sit at the top of the tree. The office youngsters dash off when the clock strikes six, others head home to get the kids in bed, then all of a sudden it's 11pm and you're working crazy hours for the third time in a week.

This isn't healthy or sustainable. As mentioned in Principle 1, hustle is not a strategy. And if the wheels would genuinely fall off if you stopped, then you need to address the causes rather than perpetuate the symptoms. Okay, lecture over. I'm not your dad, but seriously, take care of yourself.

The second common objection to getting some help is a lack of headspace, specifically, not having the time to think. If ever there was a false economy, this is it. Running around like a headless chicken is rarely a winning strategy, especially when you're taking your agency into a Market of One.

Both of these objections are remarkably common. That's probably why 'putting your own oxygen mask on first' has become a cliché. But it really is good advice. People are relying on you – probably in your personal life, as well as at work.

Remember, investing in yourself is an act of leadership. By doing so, you'll significantly improve your thinking, your actions and the fortunes of your team.

Leadership in a Market of One

Hopefully the importance of your role has really landed. If so, you're ready to consider what it means to lead your agency into a Market of One. A useful starting point is to reflect on what 'happy leader' means to you. For example:

- What will it take for you to be as excited as you need to be?
- What are your strengths as a leader?
- What drains you? And where do you draw energy from?

- How will you find your own flow state and inspire your team to follow?

These kinds of questions are rarely simple. They invite you on a very personal journey. You'll need to dig deep to find your hidden drivers and address any lingering insecurities that might otherwise sabotage your progress.

This is where getting some external support can be transformative. Co:definery often provides executive coaching during implementation. In a safe space, we can help you define change, clarify the steps to get there, and then address the blockers. This is a great way of moving from scattered to gathered. And given the scale of the opportunity to create your Market of One, cultivating your sense of focus can make a dramatic difference.

Whether you work with a coach or not, don't just power through. Any internal resistance – like procrastination – can offer valuable clues. Once you slow down and tune in, you might be surprised at just how much your instincts can tell you. Keep listening and keep working through whatever's in the way.

Get aligned

Now we've focused on you, I can reveal that there's actually a missing step in 'happy leader, happy agency'. But 'happy leader, *aligned senior leadership team*, happy agency' isn't quite as snappy.

You often hear of an agency's 'mission', but not so much about the mission for a group of people within the business. This leads us to another common component of a thorough Rollout Masterplan – defining a clear mission for your board or senior leadership team.

For example, how will they collectively define their role in your newly differentiated agency? What will they need to do

PART TWO: Five principles for creating your Market of One

differently to accelerate the necessary changes? How will their respective strengths and weaknesses dovetail with one another's?

Defining a mission for your board is usually pretty straightforward. Having worked on your Market of One together, plenty of alignment is already baked in. For that reason, a single well-designed workshop should be enough.

That said, once your board's mission has been agreed, the difference between theory and practice can still trip you up. The following prompts can help them live their mission in their daily habits, beliefs and behaviours:

- How clear is each person on their individual perspective, as well as their contribution to achieving the team's goals?

- Are they all able to take stock and be radically honest about their personal capabilities, opportunities and constraints?

- How open are they to possibility and defining options for exploration?

- How effectively can they prioritize opportunities and create clear, accountable actions for themselves?

Again, additional support can be valuable here. For example, team coaching can accelerate each person's transition from 'where *I'm* going' to 'where *we're* going'.

In Co:definery's team coaching model, we underpin progress by quantitatively highlighting the gains. We do that by assessing your team's individual leadership qualities before the process and again afterwards.

The core work starts with a group workshop to co-create or refine your board's mission. Then each person has individual coaching to define their role in achieving the shared goals. The coach's overarching vantage point ensures that everyone appreciates how they all fit together. Informed by the greater good, the team sees their blockers and blind spots, so obstacles are revealed, solutions are agreed and trust is built.

Okay, shameless plug over. But whether you work with a coach or not, ensuring your board is aligned on how it will lead in a Market of One is an important accelerant of change.

Time for commercial activation

Principle 4 has described how to bring your Narrative to life. We've explored how to evidence deep differentiation throughout your agency, how to make change accountable and how you and your senior leaders must be primed and ready to implement your Rollout Masterplan.

You're now ready for Principle 5. This is all about commercial activation – it's where being in a Market of One impacts your bottom line.

Chapter 9:
Principle 5 – Reap the Rewards

Know your value and drive profitable growth.

Across the first four principles, you've embraced a better future, defined your dream, crafted your Narrative and committed to change. In this fifth and final principle, it's time for you to Reap the Rewards.

By creating a Market of One, your ideal clients will see you as meaningfully different. That earns you the right to change how you sell, which in turn creates the opportunity to price differently and command a premium.

This chapter offers clear guidance on how to make that happen. Specifically, we'll cover how you can build trust, make selling an act of service, and price in a way that consistently converts your expertise into higher margins.

Become the trusted advisor

As an agency in a Market of One, you must be confident and commercially minded. Your people need to master uncovering needs, knowing their value and charging what they're worth. For me, that's a pretty good definition of 'trusted advisor'.

Being a trusted advisor is a great example of Principle 4's commitment to Walk the Walk. Seen through the lens of your Agency Customer Experience, showing up like this is a powerful proof point of your expertise.

And as long as most agencies rely on the same outdated playbook, this behaviour will also be highly differentiating. As per Bartle Bogle Hegarty's legendary Levi's ad: 'When the world zigs, zag.' And that's exactly what you're doing. In fact, right now, how you sell is probably your most underleveraged differentiator.

Having said all that, changing how you sell isn't easy. It's another example of how fear can block your progress. Your conditioned belief in oversupply means you've spent your whole career tiptoeing around clients, nervous of the smile slipping from their faces. You tell them what they want to hear. You decline to back a great idea. You slice your fees, even before sharing them.

This mentality of keeping the client happy at all costs is only ever a short-term fix. More to the point, you're missing out on the trust-building potential of sharing difficult truths. Now, I'm as surprised as you are to find me quoting Jesus here, but as he rightly said: 'The truth will set you free.'

Once you earn the status of expert advisor, then your honest, informed opinion becomes gold. It's literally what clients are buying from you. Just like you recognizing *yourself* as 'the prize' in Chapter 3, this is an essential mindset to develop.

Focus on client success

Being seen as a trusted advisor relies on you being relentlessly focused on what's best for the client. And although it's easy to think that you are, the reality isn't so simple.

In Chapter 2, you read about the 'leaky bucket' business model, where agencies are more focused on winning clients than helping them succeed. This self-defeating short-sightedness is the polar opposite of being a trusted advisor.

I mean, if your best people are busy chasing down new-business, then who's advising your current clients? You wouldn't trust a surgeon who's more interested in your money than your stitches.

If you don't think this applies to you, then try this little test. Visit your website and count up the mentions of your agency (e.g. 'we' and 'us') vs uses of 'you' and 'your' in relation to your clients. If there are any fewer than four times more of the latter than the former, then your priorities are painfully apparent. Kudos to me for making it to Principle 5 before leaning on a tired dating analogy but talking about yourself is rarely a good look.

It's the same with your case studies. They're probably all 'we did this' and 'we did that'. It's far rarer to see 'our client's goal was…' or even 'we helped them achieve…'

These examples are granular, but they're palpable evidence of your primary focus. Being transparently self-serving confirms you're a commodity. But serving your client's interests demonstrates that you're anything but.

And if you don't see the value in that distinction, either restart from Chapter 1 or redeploy this book as a doorstop.

Search out deeper needs

While nervously placating your clients demonstrates a misplaced focus, even if you do slow down to understand their underlying needs, getting to a good place can still take some doing.

Another of David Ogilvy's reputed maxims described the problem with market research being that 'people don't think what they feel, they don't say what they think and they don't do what they say." He might equally have been talking about clients.

This isn't a criticism. It just acknowledges that clients are no less nuanced and contrary than you, me or anyone else. That's why busting a gut to only give them what they say they *want* is often less valuable than also helping them see what they *need*.

Being overly focused on 'wants' is particularly common when short-termism dominates. Much has been written about the declining average tenure of a Chief Marketing Officer, which is probably down to about 40 minutes by now. But if your neck was on the block, big-picture innovation wouldn't be top of your to-do list either. The reality is that in risk-averse situations, clients will often seek the safest option. It's better than being bold and seen as reckless, even if their outcome suffers too.

In this situation, you also being conservative may not be the best way to help. Once *everyone's* focus narrows to a tactical sliver, it's unlikely that any deeper needs will be explored. Standing together might *feel* reassuring, but not if you're both neck-deep in quicksand.

As you can imagine, playing it safe is just one reason why clients might not immediately invite you beyond the tactical. Whatever barriers you encounter, how can you seek willing ears for more strategic advice?

First and foremost, think 'prevention not cure'. Choose clients who need to go big. Or more specifically, as you develop your Proposition, define an Audience who will relish your expert guidance. Enshrine fresh thinking as a foundation of your relationship. Don't just idly yearn for them to be 'braver' – proactively make the case for ambition from day one.

Of course, the client remains the expert on their own business. So ask questions, respect their feedback and remain humble. But never forget that as a trusted advisor, your external perspective has enormous value. And it's always a good time to uncover and fix an urgent problem.

Selling as a service

When you focus on client success in this way, something profound happens: you turn selling into an act of service. Your starting point shifts from 'how can we convince them to buy', to 'are we the right people to help'. This means that persuasion is no longer your job.

Imagine you're a careers coach for teenagers leaving school. They might know their own minds, but when it comes to navigating the professional world, you're the expert in the room. Your job is to help them make good decisions, so you wouldn't encourage them to pursue a career which doesn't match their needs.

It's the same in your client conversations. Your immediate role is to consult – to listen, learn and diagnose. Your only goal is to help them get from A to B. They might have a clear view on A, on B or on neither. So work together to define where they are, where they're going and – crucially – whether or not your agency is the right one to help them get there.

Stay curious

A key tenet of selfless selling is to stay curious. Perhaps this sounds obvious, but once again, fear can easily cloud your agenda. You need to remain open to whatever truth emerges, even if it means your agency isn't right for that particular situation.

For example, if you're utterly convinced you have the right solution, it's easy to slip back into persuasion mode. Rather than asking questions to deepen your understanding, you focus on proving your point.

This is akin to leading the witness. You might feel like a hotshot lawyer who's three steps ahead, expertly manoeuvring the client towards the only *reasonable* conclusion. But actually you're hammering them with the hard sell. You're basically saying 'the answer is us… now, what was the question again?'

This is as counterproductive as it is transparent. And it certainly doesn't build trust. In fact, like any nervous please-like-me move, it only achieves the opposite.

Manage your neediness

Self-serving neediness is extremely common in how agencies sell. Happily, once again, that means avoiding becomes a handy differentiator.

To do that, it's essential you understand your power dynamic with clients, especially when you're selling. Author and sales trainer Blair Enns has a wise take on this, expressed in the following formula:

$$\text{Power} = \frac{\text{your desirability}}{\text{the desire you show}}$$

Here, your 'power' is your authority to lead the conversation. To be powerless is to be pulled from pillar to post as your client flexes their muscles. Holding onto your power means standing up for what you believe in, including your desire to help.

Your 'desirability' to the client is everything you'd expect them to get excited about – your expertise, your experience, your reputation. All the usual things.

The 'desire you show' is where things get interesting. The formula describes how your power is created by your desirability, but then diminished by the desire you show. Or to put it another way, it doesn't matter how sexy your agency is, if you're needy then you'll turn clients off.

Curb your enthusiasm

What I love about Blair's formula is that it forces us to consider what 'desire' means, how it helps and when it becomes a problem. Your enthusiasm can communicate authority or desperation, so you'd better know which is which.

If your desire is born of desperation, you'll communicate that loud and clear by not pushing back on unhelpful constraints, like silly deadlines or a lack of decision-maker access.

In contrast, if your desire is to learn, to guide and – assuming a fit is agreed – to achieve great things together, then you'll project a confident authority.

Canny clients are well-trained to notice the difference. Even the faintest whiff of neediness will understandably be used against you – not least in negotiation. The more you want their business, the less attractive the terms they can get you to accept. That's our old friend supplier conditioning again.

The big insight here is that *feeling* needy and *showing it* are very different things. You might be genuinely desperate to win, especially if you're on a losing streak, a big client's just resigned or you have a scarily empty pipeline. Even so, once you recognize your telltale behaviours, showing up needy becomes an option you can deliberately decline.

For example, what are you communicating when you spend the first five minutes of a meeting fawning over the client's *incredible* brand? You might genuinely love it, but more likely you're just kissing their arse. In which case, you're definitely giving off needy vibes. Ditto for falling over yourself to do as you're told – that's always a sign of desperation.

The aim of the game is to channel your enthusiasm towards finding a fit. Don't be our eager-to-please surgeon from the previous chapter. Show clients that your desire isn't for winning their business, it's for helping them succeed.

Assess the client's jeopardy

Being more mindful about how you come across has another useful benefit. It also helps you be more sensitive to what clients are communicating about their own enthusiasm – or lack thereof.

Think of this as *assessing the jeopardy*. This isn't the jeopardy that a needy agency feels for winning the work. Instead, you're assessing the jeopardy *the client* feels about the prospect of you leaving their selection process.

Understanding jeopardy really matters. The keener they are to work with you, the more likely you are to win and the more authority you'll take into the relationship.

Here are three methods to help you discern the client's level of commitment:

1. **Ask meta questions**: No, not 'do you want to work with us?' I mean intelligent questions that create space for inference. For example, 'How have your priorities evolved as you've met with potential agencies?' or 'What qualities were front of mind as you compiled your shortlist?' Questions that demand thoughtful answers are rich in valuable metadata.

2. **Set clear boundaries**: Standing firm on payment terms is a good example of assessing the jeopardy. For example, 'Our payment terms are 30 days. Is that acceptable?' Another example is simply standing by your pricing. In both cases, you're saying, this is us, we believe in our value and we're cool if you don't. Remember, you're *not for everyone*.

3. **Real rapport**: In all my years leading pitches, I was sometimes surprised to lose, but never surprised to win. You always know when the client is leaning in your direction. It might be obvious, like a quiet word

in a corridor, or more subtle, like an instinctive fizz of rapport. Either way, tune in and pay attention – especially when it's absent. That might mean it's time to bail.

In each case, watch and listen hard. Focus on what's *not* being said – just as you would read between the lines of a brief. Slow down, take in *all* the information and act accordingly.

Reclaim commerciality

Alongside the curiosity and authority you need to embrace selling as an act of service, another crucial trait of the trusted advisor is *commerciality*. All this really means is the ability to make a profit. But in this context, I'd also include the awareness that you and your clients *both* need to make money.

Unsurprisingly, agencies without a commercial mindset often have the lowest margins. They're always on the back foot, struggling to raise prices with existing clients and quickly dropping their rates in pursuit of new-business.

A lack of commerciality can also show up in misplaced passion. Many a project manager or subject-matter expert has been guilty of getting so excited about delivery that the commercials have taken a back seat. And in more extreme cases, agencies can even give off the air of an impoverished artist ('It's all about the work, *darling*!').

These agencies often assume that money is the domain of their finance team. But although finance manages the cash that you have, it's not their job to secure more. Finance minimizes risk, whereas commerciality seeks out opportunity.

This illustrates why being 'commercial' has more in common with client-centricity than it does with being numerate. Of course financial literacy helps, but the core behaviour is to connect what your clients need with what your agency does. It's about uncovering demand and creating value – for your clients, as well as for the agency.

Your level of commerciality has a huge impact on how you make money, particularly on how you package your services, tailor solutions and deftly navigate different pricing and negotiation scenarios to create mutual wins. These are all essential skills for the trusted advisor – even more so if yours is a project-driven agency without the comfort of retainers.

And like the broader idea of selling as a service, because so few agencies understand commerciality, showing up with this sensibility represents another opportunity for you to stand out.

This leads us neatly on to how you can apply all these ideas in the real world.

First impressions count

When you first meet a client, you've usually already made a good first impression. That could be through your agency's reputation, its marketing or perhaps just by virtue of having received a personal introduction. Your aim now is to build on that positivity.

First meetings are like unboxing videos, where people excitedly open packages and share their experience. It's a moment of truth where expectations meet reality. If your first conversation offers clients a great experience, then your potential for a strong relationship grows. And if it doesn't, then sadly you've wasted your opportunity.

Cast your mind back to the best first meetings you've had. I don't just mean when you've ultimately headed off into the sunset together. I mean where you were at your best, the conversation was meaningful and the client readily opened up.

First, let me hazard a guess at two things you *didn't* do.

Chapter 9: Principle 5 – Reap the Rewards

I doubt you opened with some clunky rapport play, like a cyber-stalked shared interest ('Did I read that you're a stamp collector? OMG, I just LOVE stamp collecting!'). Forced rapport is as transparent as gas – and just as unwelcome.

Similarly, you almost certainly didn't launch into broadcast mode and spend 45 minutes presenting at them. If you did, you'd have been talking, rather than asking then listening. Outside of a conference talk, that rarely generates much trust.

Now, let's turn to what you *did* do. Most likely, you stayed curious and started with a question, like the old skool sales classics: 'What's on your mind?' or 'What keeps you awake at night?' It did its job and you got the client talking about their problems. Nice work.

But hold your horses. These traditional questions are certainly better than boring the client with slides or trying to bullshit them into a self-serving faux-friendship. But they also have one major drawback – they signal that you're there to be briefed, not to lead. Asking to be spoon-fed won't build trust, it just sets the expectation that you'll do as you're told.

A better way of building trust is a powerful technique called 'anchor questions', part of the 'Client-Centred Thinking' curriculum from sales training experts, True & North. Anchor questions start conversations by sharing an insight in the form of a question. Asking a question means you're meeting the basic need of showing up ready to listen and learn. But embedding an insight also shows that you're not there to be spoon-fed.

As True & North's founder David Clayton puts it:

> 'Anchor questions succinctly demonstrate your informed interest in the client's world. In just a few seconds, your position of trust is a given. This strategic start makes the conversation more valuable – for them and for you.'

What I love about this technique is that your insight doesn't even need to be right. It's just your opinion, albeit one that's been carefully chosen. So even if the client corrects you, you've still shown them that you're thinking about their business.

The deeper genius of anchor questions is True & North's application of behavioural science. The so-called 'anchoring bias' describes how we all place disproportionate value on the first information we receive. So by beginning the conversation on a strategic basis, you're far more likely to have a peer-to-peer conversation. It's a far cry from a self-commoditizing request to be briefed.

Deepen your knowledge

Having started well, how do you continue to build trust while teasing out what the client really needs? In fact, you've already had a primer on this. Here's the 'Dan Sullivan question' from Principle 2:

> 'If we were having this discussion three years from today, and you were to look back over those three years to today, what has to have happened, both personally and professionally, for you to feel happy about your progress?'

Previously we applied this question to your agency, now we're directing it towards your client's ideal future. Let's recap why it's so powerful:

- **Future focused**: You're helping to uncover the client's desired destination, not just focusing on what they want right now
- **Time bound**: You're creating guardrails to help frame their response
- **Holistic**: It speaks to positive change in the personal *and* professional realm

- **Deep:** By grounding the question in happiness, you're exploring emotional motivations that often run deeper than practical goals.

Starting with this question is the embodiment of staying curious. I mean, the client could want literally *anything* at this stage. By proactively inviting that possibility, you're firmly rejecting the temptation to crowbar your square peg into the round hole of their immediate needs. This is *seriously* selfless selling.

Symptoms, problems and solutions

Once you've asked the Dan Sullivan question, as a client-centric, consultative diagnostician, your next responsibility is to discern the depth of their understanding.

Specifically, is the client focused on the symptoms they're experiencing, the underlying problem or the overarching solution?

This is why casual questions like 'what keeps you awake at night?' can be unhelpful – they often invite superficial answers. For instance, a lack of onsite conversion might well be the immediate symptom, but without understanding the underlying cause, your solution risks being shallow and ineffective.

Your client's remit and seniority can also limit their ability to address – or even express – an underlying problem or an appropriate response. But remember your job isn't just to find an immediate need and meet it. Unless you slow down and dig deeper, you risk missing a more impactful requirement. That's a disservice to both of you.

Understand the plan

Once you're clear what the client is trying to achieve, move on to how advanced their existing plans might be. Helpful questions include:

- What approaches are you considering to achieve that?
- What have you tried in the past? What happened?
- How far down the line are you?

As well as understanding their current progress, confidence and sophistication, you're also building a picture of where they *don't* need support from you. This is valuable intel because it avoids you wasting time, effort and credibility. If it ain't broke, don't fix it.

Timing is also a smart data point to pin down. On the face of it, the following is just a simple timing question (another pearl from True & North's Client-Centred Thinking), but in fact it's all about accountability:

> 'If you started next week, when would you need to see the impact?'

This uncovers useful information about the clients' intended timeline, including contingencies or dependencies that you might not have known about. Crucially, you're also getting an implicit commitment that these timings matter.

So when your proposal gets ghosted or you're chasing next steps, rather than relying on a tepid 'any news yet?', you now have a far more compelling accountability card to play:

> 'You said you needed to see the impact by June, but we're already two weeks behind the timeline we agreed. Shall we replan together?'

Instead of just urging the client forward in service of your own agenda, you're demonstrating that you have their back.

With all of your questions, listen hard to the answers. Hone in on the emotion and where the stakes feel highest. The good stuff is always in the details, so keep playing back what you hear, checking whether you've understood correctly and asking what you've missed. Unhurried diligence is the hallmark of a professional.

Prioritize real needs

Despite having avoided the trap of trying to fix what's not broken, in large agencies in particular, there's still a constant temptation to throw *everything but the kitchen sink* at every opportunity.

This is understandable. If your tool shed is bursting with options and you don't know what the client will value, it's a comfort blanket to serve the full house with all the toppings. And like mixing three metaphors in one sentence, what you offer them will be hard to digest.

So how can you only include what the client really needs and leave out everything else? By finding out what they'd most value.

You're probably familiar with the age-old model of 'features, advantages and benefits'. A feature is what you do, its advantage is what the client gets and the benefit is why they care.

Using this model to discuss possible solutions, you might say something like 'We could do [feature], which is useful because [advantage] and then you would get [benefit]'. And because it's logical and chronological, it all feels very sensible.

Unfortunately, the benefit only appears at the end. So you're asking the client to hold a lot of information before they know whether they should care. This mistake is particularly common now that technology infuses so many agency capabilities. Like a product manual authored by an engineer, figuring out the benefits can feel too much like hard work.

A more effective method is to ask 'need-payoff questions,' a technique from Neil Rackham's book, *SPIN Selling*. Here you simply ask about *benefits*. And only if they land do you explain the associated features and advantages. For example:

- How would it impact ROI if you improved your Net Promoter Score by 5%?
- Would it be valuable if your customers could call you from within your app?
- How would it help if you could upskill your internal team?

Using need-payoff questions is like having a time machine. You get to visit the client's imagined future and see whether what you have in mind will help them get there. If it won't, that's fine, just move on and try another idea.

Uncovering precisely what your client really values – and what they don't – neatly avoids hit-and-hope proposals, 200-slide pitch decks and the depleting fear of barking up the wrong tree. See what happens to your conversion rate too.

Mind your motivation

By now, your conversation is really flying. So it's a good time to check in with your motivation. If you haven't quite banished your scarcity mindset, it's easy to lapse back into asking questions that damage your credibility.

Cast your mind back to the 'power' formula and how neediness harms your credibility. Below are standard qualifying questions that we've all asked a million times. After each one is the underlying neediness that clients are trained to spot:

1. Who are we up against? ('We're shitting ourselves about the prospect of pitching against certain agencies, so please reassure us.')
2. What are your payment terms? ('We're going to accept what you tell us because we're too scared to state what we think is acceptable.')

3. What's your budget? ('We're not the experts here, so we'll work to whatever you say, and frankly, we'll take whatever we can get.').

Instead, try these alternatives on for size:

1. How broad a range of agencies are you considering? ('Understanding how settled you are on your selection criteria means we can offer valuable insights based on our extensive experience.')

2. Our payment terms are 30 days. Is that acceptable? ('We're seeking a grown-up and respectful partnership… are you?')

3. Are you happy for me to get a little deeper into the conversation and then offer you some broad budget ranges to check that we're on the same page? ('As experts, once we know whether we can help, we'll share some indicative pricing so we can agree whether you have the budget required.').

Obviously these questions are just a representative sample of what you might typically ask. And the subsequent conversations and underlying implications will vary from client to client. The point is that to stand in your power as an expert advisor, you need to be mindful about what you're *communicating*, not just what you're *saying*.

Asking about budgets

Having raised the delicate matter of budgets, let's dig a little deeper. Not least because, as mentioned in the section about commerciality, money is an essential conversation topic for the trusted advisor.

Delay talking cash at your peril. The last thing you want to do is invest your heart and soul in a pitch, only to find that the client wants Ferrari quality for Hyundai money.

Obviously just guessing about budgets isn't helpful, so asking is better than nothing. But a direct question like 'how much budget is set aside?' will often only get you an annoyingly unhelpful answer, like 'just give us some options' or 'we'd rather not say'.

Instead, once you have a detailed sense of what the client needs, you can take the initiative and share what *you* think their budget needs to be. You'll be surprised how much more responsive they are. This is why offering ranges rather than specific numbers really helps. It gives the client more space to respond with gentle guidance, like 'it had better be closer to the lower end' or 'that doesn't sound too far off'.

Even indirect feedback speaks volumes, like a raised eyebrow, widening of the eyes or a sharp intake of breath. As a professional seller, that's all the invitation you need to enquire further. Likewise, the absence of pushback – subtle or explicit – suggests tacit acceptance that you're in the right ballpark. They might not want to give you a fixed number, but they also don't want to waste their time.

Taking the lead in the money conversation improves your odds and demonstrates your professionalism. And once again, because so few agencies do it, it's yet another opportunity to be perceived as different.

Earn trust by mitigating risk

Having invested the time to understand what the client really needs and how much they might pay, the last thing you want is to be derailed at the final pitch stage – not least by a thorny question that you failed to anticipate.

We've all been there. For weeks you work crazy-long hours, and the big day finally arrives. The work is strong, the deck looks great and you're feeling confident. A canny colleague finds some weaknesses in your solution, so you prepare strong responses in case the client spots them too.

Back in the day, we called these 'killer questions'. We'd figure out what they might be, who would answer them and how best to deflect the danger. I mean, talk about *defensive* – this is not what being in a Market of One is all about.

So rather than defend your vulnerabilities, why not just be more robust? Need-payoff questions were a great place to start because they uncovered benefits that you know the client values. Now step two is to deal with risks early, rather than hoping they stay hidden until the end.

To do that, here's another powerful tool: the pre-mortem. This is a project management technique where imagining failure is the basis for predicting what might go wrong.

Applying this to sales is another innovation from the smart folk at True & North. Instead of letting *unknown* unknowns cause problems later, you proactively seek out risks at the start, so that you and the client can address them together.

True & North's founder David Clayton describes why the timing matters:

> 'In that moment when the client says "write me a proposal", instead of skipping off and doing exactly that, a pre-mortem offers you a robust and intuitive way to lean in, partner with the client and explore what might go wrong.'

Perhaps raising risks feels awkward or even foolhardy, but remember your job is to diagnose a fit. If you and the client are on the same page, then why wouldn't they agree to invest a little time exploring what's in the way of success?

And if they're reluctant, it's a timely clue that you might not be as aligned as you thought. It's far better to know that now rather than only finding out once your pitch comes 'a close second'.

So take a deliberate walk through the minefield of the client's stakeholders and their respective concerns. Uncover who's involved, what's on their mind and how you might improve your chances of shared success. Agree your collective priorities, actions and plan of attack.

Unlike fielding killer questions, seeking out risk is an act of diligence, not self-preservation. Instead of protecting weakness, you're projecting confidence. Better still, a pre-mortem often reveals opportunities to make your solution even better. And all the while, you're already working side-by-side with the client, despite the pitch still being weeks away.

As with all of Principle 5, you're partnering with your client to steward their ideal future into being. You're earning the role of trusted advisor.

Ditch the big reveal

Once you make it to pitch day you have the opportunity to sidestep another bear trap in agencies' generic playbook – the big reveal.

Too many pitches follow the turgid tradition of playing back the brief, banging on about how detailed your research has been, and only then getting to the substance of what you're actually recommending. I mean, seriously?

And don't get me started on a lack of signposting. At least a decent contents slide warns the client how much meandering they need to endure before you get to the good stuff.

One alternative is to use a version of 'card sorting'. You collate all the topics, ask the client where they want to start and take it from there. What could've been yet another one-way broadcast becomes an organic, co-creative conversation. As well as being memorable, you're also demonstrating your flexibility – and your command of the material.

Another technique is the 'advocate's approach'. I learned this from a former mentor of mine, ex-Interpublic Chief Growth Officer Kevin Allen and his book, *The Hidden Agenda*. In essence, you treat the pitch like you would a courtroom trial. Just as a lawyer *starts* with their big reveal – an assertion of guilt or innocence – you begin with your own. Then everything that follows serves as evidence. This affords you all manner of opportunities to weave in engaging plot twists, but the whole story is anchored in the core idea that you led with.

To reprise the notion of you zagging while the world zigs, doing anything that breaks the monotony of the undifferentiated will be welcomed with open arms.

You're always selling 'value'

Having explored selling from the perspective of being in a Market of One, you might expect a section on 'value' to be a predictable segue into pricing. You'd only be half right.

Before we get into that most tangible point of difference, we need to talk about an elephant in the room: the widely misunderstood subject of 'value'. Specifically, some unhelpful definitions, as well as a lack of self-belief.

Value isn't skin in the game

Unhelpful definition number one is equating 'value' with performance-related pay. This is bizarrely common, not least in the widely used – but rarely applied – term, 'value-based pricing'. If I had a pound for every time I'd heard this, I'd have an even more debilitating trainer habit (that's 'sneakers' to you, American friends).

Value-based pricing simply means agreeing a price based on the client's perception of value. But whether that price then varies in line with certain metrics is an entirely separate question – albeit one that can be complementary.

This isn't some arcane nuance. When a healthy conversation about value casually slips into one about skin in the game, it tends to end there. This is hardly surprising. Most agencies are wary of hazy attribution and few clients are enthusiastic about budget uncertainty. Before you know it, a progressive road closes and you're back to selling time like everyone else (more on that shortly).

Value isn't always an outcome

It's similarly limiting to define 'value' solely as an outcome. This makes 'value' synonymous with 'objective', like an improvement in sales, cost-per-acquisition or brand recall. These are fine as goals but viewing 'value' only as an end result is unhelpfully narrow.

As an agency, you offer almost unlimited flavours of value. Access to certain talent? One concept or three? Unlimited amends? Insights only or recommendations too? Working prototypes? Positive campaign pre-test? Sign-off from the client's board? Experience? Credibility? Speed? Money-back guarantee? You name it.

And so it goes on. Value is personal to all of us. It all depends on what any given client actually needs – and how well you've understood their underlying drivers.

Embrace subjectivity

The infinite subjectivity of value also informs your own sense of self-worth, and with it, your ability to command a premium. If you don't believe your agency is *worth* more, then how will you *charge* more?

Remember that being a commodity makes you indistinguishable other than by price. You may have noticed that's not fun. So as you step beyond that world, recognize that your work is like art, property or precious stones – if people pay handsomely and walk away happy, then that's what it's worth. That's not profiteering – it's a win-win.

At the end of the day, price and expectation offer no guarantees, so we all invest based on perception. A gig ticket for a living legend might cost you the earth and leave you disappointed. Or perhaps you pay pennies to see an unknown artist and the music blows you away.

That's just how buying stuff works. It's not about *why* things cost what they cost, it's whether you feel you got value for money. The operative – and subjective – word is 'feel'.

It's the same with agency value. At the end of the day, clients need your talent and motivation – neither of which can be standardized in a rate card or by benchmarking deliverables. And if you don't believe that, then it's unlikely that they will either.

All hail value-based selling

These misunderstandings obscure the fact that everything you say and do – especially when you're selling – should be designed to uncover and create client-specific value.

That's why I'd argue that 'value-based selling' is the most inclusive and far-reaching context for 'value'. Whether you define that as consultative selling, solution selling or whatever else it's been described as over the years, the key point is that it's incumbent on you as an expert to listen first, and then carefully offer a tailored solution built around what that particular client values.

This is the embodiment of being a trusted advisor. It's also the basis for believing in what you do, enjoying your work and leveraging your uniqueness to command a premium.

PART TWO: Five principles for creating your Market of One

Commanding a premium

So, with value defined, let's talk about how you get paid more. This book is structured very deliberately. As mentioned at the start of this chapter, first you need to be different. That earns you the right to sell differently. And only then can you successfully charge more. Trying to command a premium in any other order is far less likely to succeed.

You might remember Belgian lager Stella Artois' famous strapline, 'Reassuringly Expensive'. If their branding wasn't upmarket and the beer tasted like piss, for them to command a price premium would've just been wishful thinking.

Contrast Stella's confidence with the typical agency attitude to selling and pricing, which is to aim for competitor parity. Pitches follow the rulebook. And instead of pricing being an opportunity to stand out, it's a fearful rush to comply. Remarkably, agencies even like to benchmark themselves via their trade bodies, as if to save procurement the hassle. Go figure.

Like so much of this book, these habits speak to culture, commoditization and the fear of losing opportunities. But as an agency in a Market of One, once you see these behaviours as *choices*, then you can improve how you sell, change how you price and sustain a far healthier bottom line than your competitors.

Costing is a science, pricing is an art

As a case in point, the story at the start of Principle 4 described a world-class agency that failed to translate its success into any kind of premium. Sadly, this isn't unusual. So what can you do about it?

One reason even in-demand agencies struggle to improve their margins is because they hold rigid views about cost and price.

These views are enshrined in the industry-wide default to selling time. If you're keen to evolve how you price – and please tell me you are – then this is well worth unpacking.

No-one has more helpfully described the cost-vs-price dynamic than consultant and pricing maestro Tim Williams. I once saw him present at a conference and he made the point that costing is a tactical calculation, but pricing is a strategic judgement. Or to put it another way, while costing is a science, pricing is an art. Most agencies default to the former without exploiting the latter.

Tim elegantly highlighted how pricing should work in precisely the reverse order of the traditional agency costing process.

With costing, you begin with your solution, use fixed-margin day-rates to arrive at your price, then you work hard to convince the client of its value.

In contrast, the art of pricing works the other way. You start with what the client values. Then you put a number against it. And only then do you assess the 'cost', i.e. the solution you can afford to build – and crucially, how much margin you choose to make.

In the traditional cost-first approach, you're playing catch-up, hoping to persuade the client that the value of your solution matches its price tag. Given tight purse strings, procurement power and the weight of subjectivity, that's a tough ask.

But in the more progressive price-first model, everything builds from your skilful diagnosis. You find out what the client needs and what it's worth to them, and then you take it from there.

Of these two approaches, you can see which one is the easier sell. That's another reason why being a trusted advisor is so foundational.

PART TWO: Five principles for creating your Market of One

Goodbye time

Understanding the cost-vs-price dynamic is a helpful stepping stone into a world beyond day-rates. Which is good news because the AI revolution is shaking everyone – including clients – out of their slumber on pricing.

As machines increasingly handle the legwork you used to charge for, selling time will become a quaint custom we'll look back on with bemusement, like rewinding VHS tapes before returning them to Blockbuster.

And selling time is already problematic. For a start, it's hampered by an inherent lack of scalability. To make more money, you need more people. Which is a pretty unnecessary constraint to impose on your own profitability. In fairness, you can also raise your day-rates, but that's a tough sell across your entire client base, so it's often only an incremental gain.

Another issue with selling time is that the incentives are woefully misaligned. Why would anyone want a system where speed is actively discouraged? As legendary Chief Marketing Officer David Wheldon OBE once told me: 'Clients are paying agencies to get it wrong, when it would cost them less if they got it right.'

It seems like the only argument in favour of hourly rates is the success of our friends in the legal trade. They click their little clocks like chess players, logging every second that they're on your dime. Their work takes as long as it takes and you're left dreading their invoice, knowing only that you'll be charged for every minute, regardless of the outcome or whether they even broke into a sweat.

But let's get real. Lawyers' earning power isn't really about pricing models. Although they're far better than agencies at tracking and recovering their time, their real strength is being specialized professionals solving high-stakes problems. Now, why does that sound familiar?

Start with fixed pricing

As agency leaders look to improve their margins, they often ask me which innovative new pricing techniques will emerge to replace selling time. My answer is dull but honest: agencies will be using the same models that you already use at home.

Just check out your credit card statement. You'll find dynamic pricing from airlines, cab firms and your energy company. You'll see subscriptions for everything from printer ink to car maintenance. Even your local sandwich shop offers you a discount for committing your monthly spend up front. And although your coffee machine was a bargain, the pods cost an arm and a leg.

If you are taking your first steps beyond selling time, then charging fixed prices for specific deliverables is a great place to start. Think of this as base camp on your journey to having a modern, multifaceted suite of pricing models.

Philosophically, fixed price is a massive leap forward. Instead of fighting to justify what you're doing (i.e. spending X hours on Y service), you're selling what the client actually gets. No wonder, then, that there are some subtleties to be mindful of.

For example, most software companies offer fixed prices, but their costs are also pretty fixed once their products go live. So given that agency solutions can vary massively, how can you avoid making the painful mistake of your costs exceeding your price?

The simple answer is to use your expertise, the essence of which is 'pattern matching'. This is your ability to draw on your knowledge and experience to make better decisions. Over time, you'll develop a deep reservoir of trust in yourself. The more you see a similar problem, the better you can anticipate the right approach to fixing it. That's as true of agencies as it is for medics, mechanics or midwives.

Of course this takes some time. But remember you're not starting from scratch – you already know a lot. More to the point, you're also deliberately designing your Market of One around your deepest expertise.

By combining demonstrable knowledge with your trusted advisor skillset, you have everything you need to uncover – and monetize – the nuanced value that each client perceives.

So of course every challenge is different. But each one will offer similarities. And instead of fearing the variation of infinite solutions, celebrate your ever-expanding capacity to adapt to the details. Any nervousness will soon be overwritten by your burgeoning superpowers – as well as a serene sense of confidence. This is what deep expertise feels like.

Rejecting like-for-like

You might worry that adopting fixed pricing makes you just as easy to compare – and beat up – as selling time. In effect, you're swapping one subjective proxy (units of time) for another (units of stuff).

For example, being told that your concept fee or discovery phase is 50% more expensive than your competitor's may feel just as problematic as hearing that your day-rates differ to the same degree.

The solution here is to stop pretending that subjectivity doesn't exist. Instead, you need to advocate for its importance. During my agency career, I quite enjoyed this philosophical debate with clients and procurement people. It was an opportunity to demonstrate belief in the value my agency was bringing, as well as in our willingness to walk away.

The basic exchange was a pretty classic power struggle:

- [Me]: So, that's the price for our deliverable.
- [Client]: What are your hours and rates?

- [Me]: Sorry, we don't work like that.
- [Client]: But how did you arrive at the number?
- [Me]: Experience, mainly. Does it matter?
- [Client]: Well, we need to compare you on a like-for-like basis with the other agencies.
- [Me]: Is that so it's easier for you to negotiate us down?
- [Client]: Well, yes.
- [Me]: And why would I do that?
- [Client]:
- [Me]: Are you still there? Hello?

Now, I appreciate that you may not yet have the confidence to stand your ground like this. But it's important you see this ridiculous dynamic for what it is. While buyers will always want to commoditize you, it's up to you whether you let them. Seriously, why would you?

Remember the idea of 'assessing the jeopardy'? If the client is nervous of your unique solution being whisked away, then you'll earn the compromise you wanted. Alternatively, if they're not especially bought into what you're offering, then they'll hold their ground, so you can call out the lack of fit and decide to step away. Either way, you're one step closer to a right-fit client who genuinely needs what you do.

Once you're in a Market of One, you can consistently enter these conversations knowing your worth. Having elevated your sales process to a highly personalized collaboration, you know that however the client responds will strengthen your resolve.

Most importantly, you're now more than happy to walk away from a wrong-fit client. And you're no longer compelled to join your competitors in their ruinous race to the bottom.

PART TWO: Five principles for creating your Market of One

Always explore options

Whether you're selling time, fixed price or anything else, how you present your pricing is mission critical. Even at this late stage in the sale, you're still discerning value – by offering options and talking them through.

If you're a fan of behavioural science, you'll recognize the concept of 'choice architecture' here. You're carefully designing the environment in which the client makes their decision about whether to hire your agency.

You're not channelling them towards one option over another. You're just presenting information in a way that makes it easier for them to discern what they need.

Going for gold, silver or bronze

These days, options are literally everywhere in selling. From popcorn at the movies to milkshakes at McDonalds, we're so used to being given choices that we barely notice. And in the B2B world that agencies operate in, the undisputed champions of choice architecture are software companies.

As I sit here and type, I can see icons for Hubspot, Mailchimp, Xero and Typeform, all of whom offer so-called 'tiered' pricing. You might characterize this as 'gold, silver, bronze' pricing, just like a car wash. Bronze is the basic wash, silver might include your wheels and then gold adds in a cheeky polish. As you move up through the tiers, each price point becomes more seductive and feels more foolish to ignore.

From an agency perspective, your pricing tiers operate like the bespoke packages and products described in the previous chapter. By bundling deliverables at different price points, you're emphasizing your specialization. You can also include fully formed products within your tiers to increase the uniqueness of your solution.

Pricing in tiers also thwarts like-for-like comparison between your specialist apples and your competition's generalist oranges. And it helps you deflect invasive enquiries into how much money you make or how you make it. After all, when you buy a laptop, you don't ask the retailer how much they paid for the battery.

All this keeps the conversation focused on what the client gets, how they benefit and what the associated price will be. You're diligently helping them explore what's in each tier, whether each component is needed and even what might need to be added.

Your conversation concludes with an agreed set of options that reflect exactly what the client needs. This can then be written up as a statement of work that you're both already happy with, ready for immediate sign-off.

Make sure you're in the room

Before we move on, it's important to emphasize that managing choice means controlling the *entire* environment. So as well as presenting options, you also need to tightly manage how and when the client sees them.

Talking options through is essential. So make it clear that your options document is a discussion guide, not a proposal. It requires a live conversation, not a back and forth over email. Ideally you'll be in the same room or at the very least on video conference.

With that use case established, you also need to control access to your options. Treat the following advice as gospel:

- Don't share your options ahead of time, even if the client asks nicely
- If the big cheese can't make it, ideally reschedule or at least hold a second meeting

- When you're meeting face-to-face, use the big screen rather than handouts
- If you're dialling in, use screen share rather than emailing your options.

All this might sound a bit extreme, especially if the client gets heavy-handed. But don't be deterred from standing your ground.

Decline unhelpful requests with gentle clarity. It's just part and parcel of how you work. Explain that the value of options comes from the conversation they provoke. You're enabling the client to define precisely what they need and how much they want to spend. In this context, you leaving their interpretation open to chance would be irresponsible.

And don't be shy in acknowledging that this approach works better for you too. You're here for the win-win and exploring subjectivity together helps everyone.

Honestly, pricing – like so much of selling – is really just a dance. So smile, have fun and enjoy it together.

Working with procurement

That nearly concludes your reinvention of selling and pricing. All that remains is the small matter of client-side procurement. Having already covered their influence and tactics in Part One, the last point to cover is your reluctance to say no to them.

When I stopped being an agency employee, I started meeting procurement people outside of a negotiation context. Can I share a secret? They were universally lovely. Not Rottweilers, nor heartless bastards. Who knew?

What surprised me was their disappointment that agencies don't put up more of a fight. Just like you, these are professional people seeking professional fulfilment. But when agencies meekly surrender their margins, that offers procurement folk about as much satisfaction as shooting fish in a barrel. With an assault rifle.

A procurement person once told me that his job was to ask agencies for concessions until they say no. He went on to offer an important tip – rather than just comply until you crumble, if you just said no sooner, it would cut short the whole process.

So if you don't like what procurement is asking, then just say no. It's as simple as that, regardless of the size of the prize or the stage in the process. At the very least, saying no can be the first step towards collaborating on an alternative.

Even just the idea of pushing back often makes agency folk nervous. They cite commercial pressures and needing revenue to avoid layoffs, but that's a short-sighted view. You don't make money by signing bad deals. And if your agency's in a tight spot, then your problem lies well upstream of procurement.

Ultimately it's your responsibility to defend your commercial interests. And once you can confidently explain how they align with the client's own priorities, then you have every right to stand your ground. Believe in yourself and the value of your expertise.

At the same time, if the gloves do come off and a brutal procurement person asks you to do something that's fundamentally opposed to what you believe in, then it's an even easier 'no'. You either have principles or you don't. And believe me, your team is watching with interest.

Make friends not enemies

Here's one last thought on procurement. In amongst all this 'just say no' – why not just say 'hello'? Might it be helpful to have friendlier, more open relationships with procurement people? Revolutionary, I know.

For the majority of agencies, proactively engaging procurement represents an untapped opportunity. Conversing outside of the confines of a formal selection process can be game-changing. There's just so much to learn and share.

Launching your new Proposition? See what your mate in procurement makes of it. Looking to productise your services? Give them a call. Keen to understand their incentives and buying criteria? You know what to do.

Step up and lead

This fifth and final principle is about reaping the rewards of being in your Market of One. By making client success your primary focus, you're translating differentiation into an ability to command a premium.

Being paid to provide guidance is a noble duty. Experts tell clients what they need to know, not just what they want to hear. Of course there's a subtle art to choosing your words and picking your moment, but that's the diplomacy you learn as you embed the practice and your confidence grows.

Changing the dynamic with your existing clients won't always be easy, but every new prospect is an opportunity to start afresh. Your new-found combination of genuine differentiation and selfless selling gives you all the permission you need to have a deeper conversation.

And once you're welcomed into a more trusted relationship, you become an indispensable advisor. Genuine partnership and healthy profit margins will follow.

This is what it means to be in a Market of One. You'll unlock the joy of doing the most fulfilling and lucrative work of your career.

PART THREE:
Choosing to thrive

Chapter 10:
Address the hurdles

Part Two detailed the five principles for creating your Market of One. Part Three is all about accelerating your progress.

At its heart, this book offers you a simple choice. You can keep ploughing the dusty wasteland of oversupply. Or you can farm the fertile ground of deep differentiation.

The former is hard graft but offers the comfort of familiarity. The latter promises a richer future but brings with it the inherent uncertainty of the new. Stick or twist. The age-old dilemma.

By now you should feel like there's no choice at all.

The agency industry is poised for transformation. But let's be honest, it was ever thus. You can take your place at the forefront – or you can be left behind. And to be frank, if you continue to behave like a commodity, then you'll only have yourself to blame as you watch others prosper.

Unsurprisingly, my advice would be to step up.

But in case you're not quite ready, this chapter is designed to address any remaining resistance. Here are the most common objections from agencies who've stood in your shoes before creating their own Market of One.

Objection 1: There's no such thing as a Market of One

When people question whether a Market of One is even possible, it's more an outright rejection than a specific objection. It boils down to Principle 1 not having landed – they don't yet Believe in Better.

As you've read, to Believe in Better is a call to arms, as well as a non-negotiable starting point. So what if you're not there yet?

In fairness, unshakeable positivity might not arise overnight, especially if the Big Grind is the only world you know. That's okay – it just means your early steps might be a little tentative.

The underlying leap is to choose to be the master of your own destiny. Conforming to unwritten rules and dated conventions is a joyless existence. It's also a slippery slope to a place you really don't want to be. Make no mistake, this isn't a simple choice of believing in better or staying where you are. Your ship is already sinking.

So listen, I'm not here to persuade you. If you've gotten this far through your career – and this book – and don't recognize the commercial benefits of lasting differentiation, then let's just agree to differ.

My only invitation is to pause and look around you. See which agencies are doing well and reflect on why that might be. In fairness, being in a Market of One goes beyond profile and reputation, so awarding the accolade from a distance is like judging a house by looking through the keyhole. But even so, it's worth seeking out some inspiration.

And if you still don't believe that differentiation powers the world's best-performing agencies, then I'd love to discuss that with you. Similarly, if all you see is a sea of sameness and you still choose to tread water, then I salute your stamina if not your logic.

In either case, feel free to give this book away. In fact, by all means hand it to someone you'd like to fail, like your biggest competitor. That'll show 'em.

Objection 2: There aren't enough 'markets' for everyone

Some leaders worry that there simply can't be enough 'markets of one' for every agency. This objection tends to come up early or not at all. It's usually accompanied with a quizzical eyebrow and takes the form of a question that begins with 'surely...'

If this is on your mind, you might also feel a wistful sense of 'I'd *like* to believe, but...' This is just your conditioning talking. It's a life spent on the front lines of commoditization, searching for mythical 'unique selling points' that don't sound like bullshit bingo.

Remember that your Market of One is crafted from what makes you unique. This includes your expertise, experiences and beliefs, not to mention your culture and collective aspirations. These qualities are like a fingerprint: fundamentally, scientifically and unarguably *yours*.

Once you liberate yourself from the herd mentality, you'll see that no two agencies are any more alike than any two people. By shedding your identical packaging, your opportunity for uniqueness is infinite – as is your ability to evolve over time.

So, could literally *everyone* have a Market of One? In theory, yes. But as US baseball coach Yogi Berra reputedly said: 'In theory, there's no difference between theory and practice, but in practice, there is.'

First of all, although there are a *lot* of agencies, there's also a truck-load of money to play for. Industry measurement body WARC predicted that global advertising spend would top $1 trillion for the first time in 2024, with additional rises forecasted in 2025 and 2026 to take the total market to $1.24 trillion. And remember that's just the media pot.

But whether there's enough money to go round really isn't the point. The reality is that many agencies simply won't make the leap. To coin a phrase, a Market of One *isn't for everyone* – philosophically, anyway. Hence Objection 1.

The Darwinian truth is that forward-thinkers will specialize and squeeze out the undifferentiated stragglers. This will prompt more of the latter to change, but by then they'll be playing catch-up. Choose your cohort wisely.

Objection 3: Our clients won't like it

This is a concern that your clients will reject your newly differentiated agency. It takes us back to Stockholm Syndrome – if you've become sympathetic to your captors' priorities, then it makes sense that change makes you nervous.

Notice the status quo that you're instinctively protecting. How's it working for you so far? And how will it play out? If you keep giving clients free rein, they'll keep demanding more and more for less and less. So maybe breaking a few norms needn't feel so disruptive?

To get further into this, what do you imagine your clients will push back on? Here are the most common examples:

- **Changing your Proposition**: The concern is that your current clients will leave in droves if they no longer feel your offer represents their needs. But remember that not only did you involve clients in your journey, your Market of One also accentuates your existing strengths. So they're more likely to be thrilled than jump ship. And even if you pivot further than Michael Jordan becoming a librarian, any clients who take offence would be the ones you'd happily replace anyway.

- **Selling differently**: Apparently the rules of new-business were chiselled into tablets of stone and handed down unto agencies at the foot of a sacred mountain. Such is the unwavering regard in which they're held. I call bullshit. Healthy selling is helpful selling. The habitual failure to listen, learn and advise is madness. It's a disservice to your clients and it's a disservice to your bottom line. Good clients will welcome your diligence.

- **Alternative pricing models**: The need to atomize your pricing into like-for-like fragments is just a procurement-spun fable. The notion that this is the only way clients buy would be laughable if it wasn't so universally believed. It's sacrilege, I know, but you *do* need to make money. Weak margins mean weak talent, which means weak work. Everybody loses, including clients.

At the heart of all these examples is fear. The idea that your clients will reject your new strategy is a knee-jerk demonstration of that stubborn scarcity mindset. But once you step into your Market of One, hearing the word 'no' is actually what you want. It means you're standing your ground, fighting for what you believe in and earning the client's trust.

When you hold firm with calmness and good humour, you'll open up more productive conversations. And whenever you reach an impasse with a client who isn't a good fit, just smile and walk away – then take your team down the pub. These are the culture-building 'wins' they'll talk about for years.

Objection 4: I'm too busy to change

We've all been here. Business isn't perfect, but it's okay. Changing things up would be great, but the main hurdle is the endless firefighting. Like a creaky old rollercoaster, things are moving fast, but you don't quite feel in control.

PART THREE: Choosing to thrive

This is the classic important vs urgent dynamic. But when *everything* feels urgent and important, you slide into overwhelm.

No doubt being in a Market of One sounds great in theory – better clients, better margins, more time and money to hire and develop better people. It's just that… wait, the phone's ringing again. And so it goes on.

Unfortunately, as you know, being crazy busy isn't the same as making progress. You're doing enough to survive, but not enough to thrive. Often it's the smaller opportunities that convert. With the larger ones, you keep coming a close second. Some money's coming in, but the toll is high. You and your team are exhausted. The return on energy invested isn't enough.

This places you in the danger zone. Too many agencies avoid questions of strategy and differentiation until they're struggling. They only commit to change once they've hit the wall – emotionally, as well as commercially. Then they're facing a turnaround job – more urgent, higher risk and far harder to do.

So listen, I get it. The sense of impossibility feels real. But the hardest part is choosing to step off the treadmill. It's not really about being too busy - it's about being motivated enough to set priorities. Forgive the crude analogy, but you're never too busy to find time to use the toilet.[1]

The best advice I can offer is to be mindful of the risks and don't wait for a crisis. Change will only get harder. Now might be a good time to check out Co:definery's Diagnostic Questionnaire at www.codefinery.com/dq

Objection 5: This feels scarily narrow

This objection reflects the deep-seated concern that specialization must be 'narrow', which feels risky and restrictive.

---

[1] Blame Tony Robbins for that, I stole it from him.

But as you read in Chapter 3, to 'specialize' doesn't have to mean limiting your agency to a single discipline or a single vertical. In fact, unless you specialize in something, then you don't have a business strategy at all.

Remember that the world's most broadly skilled marketing services holding companies are highly specialized. Global advertisers who want a one-stop shop only have a handful of options to choose from. Being specialized changes the power dynamic – it reduces the client's leverage and increases yours.

Nervousness about narrowness is scarcity talking once again. It's the worry that being more focused means declining vast swathes of inbound new-business that you're no longer willing to accept. That's a bowl full of spaghetti's worth of tangled thinking.

Most obviously, if you're currently enjoying these 'vast swathes' of opportunities, then why change anything? But back in the real world, we're back to the age-old misconception that being all things to all people is the best way to accelerate growth. Once again, that just doesn't hold water. You'd never recommend your clients cast their marketing net so indiscriminately, so don't fall into that trap yourself.

A more valid concern about 'narrowness' is ensuring that your chosen Market of One offers enough commercial opportunity to realize your Vision. That's precisely why the five principles are grounded in iteration, validation and flexibility. If you convene smart people, follow a proven process and course correct as you power ahead, you won't be left wondering where the money is.

Objection 6: My agency is too big

Unsurprisingly, leaders of larger agencies are the ones who worry that they're too big to create a Market of One. This concern usually takes one of two forms: being too big to change or too big to focus. There's a dangerous grain of truth in both, so let's unpack each in turn.

If you're running a multinational agency, being 'too big to focus' can feel very real. As well as echoing the previous objection around 'narrowness', there's also a confronting reality that big agencies rarely have much of an ownable Vision.

No doubt you have the usual financial targets and woolly aspirations. But this isn't enough. As you read in Principle 2, you need a bespoke Vision statement that goes beyond year-on-year numbers to articulate a more nuanced destination.

So while adopting this kind of focus may feel new or even politically exposing, what choice do you really have? Without a Vision, whatever 'strategy' you have has nowhere to take you. You can't plot a course if you don't have a destination. Seriously, try it on Google Maps.

Turning to the 'too big to change' concern, this can also feel worryingly real. Whether your agency is progressive and nimble, or old-fashioned and slow, it's no mean feat to retool a collection of offices, markets, offerings and sub-cultures. It's the classic cliché about turning an oil tanker. But if you're steering a skyscraper-sized vat of flammable liquid straight towards disaster, don't stress the turning circle - just yank the bloody wheel.

That's the 'just get on with it' argument. A more measured response to being 'too big' is found through the lens of change management. The rationale for creating your Market of One isn't so different from a traditional 'repositioning'. Sure, there's more provenance and culture change for you to implement, but the commercial impact of these improvements was your reason for change in the first place.

Easy? Not always. Essential? Damn right.

Objection 7: My agency is too small

The concern that your agency is too small to create a Market of One is a curious one. After all, throughout this book the most often cited 'unicorn' agencies are all independents that started small.

Even so, you might believe that fame, scale or extensive resources are prerequisites for real differentiation and lasting commercial success. Nothing could be further from the truth. All you actually need is conviction and alignment.

In truth, feeling too small is really about not feeling ready. This comes across loud and clear in a range of common excuses. Large agencies can afford to invest. Large agencies have deeper client relationships. Large agencies have a wider talent pool. And so it goes on.

The fact that these excuses aren't true is actually beside the point. If you're not a big agency, there's no sense stressing your perceived differences. Alas, I'm not as handsome, tall or talented as Harrison Ford. I've just had to get over it.

So does it help to have natural advantages? Of course it does. A contact book four inches thick? Useful. A stack of Cannes Lions in your back pocket? Very useful. High-profile founders with friends in the trade press? Definitely super useful. But these are far from mandatory conditions for following the advice in this book.

Most importantly, don't forget that you have your own unique advantages too. Recognizing and deploying them is the core of creating your Market of One. Your competitive advantage is waiting to be harnessed.

Whether your headcount is measured in thousands or on the fingers of one hand, no agency holds all the aces. So you only have two options. You can skilfully play the hand you've been dealt or you can fold. Staying in the game means you could win, leaving the table means you definitely won't.

Objection 8: It's too big a commitment

Speaking of gambling, some leaders are nervous that creating a Market of One means going all-in. This can feel reckless, like heading to Vegas and putting all your chips on red. Again, there's some truth in this – you *do* need to commit. But that's where the similarity to roulette ends.

Having a Vision and a clear strategy leaves you nowhere to hide. However consensual your leadership style, you're telling your agency, 'this is me, this is where we should go, and this is how I think we can get there'. This visibility is part and parcel of being in charge. It's why you get paid the big bucks. Pressure is a privilege and all that.

It might help to remember that you only need to be directionally correct. Implementing your Market of One won't be immediately perfect. Renowned sage and occasional boxer Mike Tyson once famously said: 'Everybody has plans until they get hit for the first time'.[2] So yes, you've gone public with your perspective on the big picture. But you don't just spin the wheel and pray, you course correct along the way.

Don't dial-up the pressure unnecessarily. Recognize the need for change, accept that the greater risk lies in inaction, and then figure out where you can win. After that, armed with conviction about your uniqueness, you have everything you need to keep learning, keep improving and keep the faith. Your job is to focus, not freeze.

---

[2] This quote's actually real! In August 1987, Mike Tyson was quoted by the Associated Press prior to his fight with Tyrell Biggs. It's unclear if Biggs had a 'plan', but he certainly lost.

Chapter 11:
Bring people with you

To get a little meta for a moment, really this whole book is designed to help you Believe in Better. Much as I'd love to imagine you've been busy creating your Market of One as you've read each chapter, it's more likely that you're reaching this point without having started in earnest.

In which case, now's a good time to emphasize the importance of collaboration. It's all very well having your own epiphany about the case for change. But whether you're managing up or managing down, yours can't be a lone voice falling on deaf ears. You need to bring people with you.

So at the risk of sounding like one of *those* planners who can't resist an esoteric reference, allow me to draw from Greek mythology. Apollo gifted Cassandra the ability to see the future, but also cursed her so that no-one would heed her warnings. Long story short, that basically sucked for her. So don't let it happen to you.

Build a coalition of the willing

You might know this lovely quote attributed to the cultural anthropologist, Margaret Mead (I got it from the NBC series,

The West Wing): 'Never doubt that a small group of thoughtful, committed citizens can change the world. Indeed, it is the only thing that ever has.'

This is remarkably good advice, so your first step is to convene your own 'small group of citizens'. This will be your coalition of the willing. They won't just help you shape your initial Vision, they'll also become your eyes and ears, your political aircover and your ambassadors for change.

Start by talking to the people who matter. Make time for a proper conversation. Be vulnerable and ask for help. Park your seniority and seek their honest opinion. Maybe share some stimulus. Give them a copy of this book. At this stage it's all about starting the conversation.

As your coalition is forming, invest the time to get everyone together. Get offsite. Switch off your bloody phones (the world won't end, I promise). Set clear expectations. Explain that you're exploring possibilities and you can't do it without them.

Frankness is mandatory. When I run these sessions, I ask everyone to imagine they've had two drinks, but no more. A two-drink vibe is passionate and engaged. Three or more and the passion might get a bit much.

Emphasize that everyone's voice matters. For one, tell them that this is their opportunity to shape the future of your agency. And even more importantly, they each have a duty to express their concerns, especially whenever they feel like the lone voice of dissent.

You also need to liberate people from their business-as-usual mindset. The ever-present pressures of hitting deadlines and delivering the numbers can make any kind of change feel impossible. To focus on the important, you all need to escape the urgent.

Similarly, be mindful that the risks you see as imminent might barely be specks on their horizons. Make your argument passionately but diligently, lest your concerns be dismissed as fear-mongering. Remember Cassandra's curse.

Power your rocket

To help you build your coalition, here's a reliable truth for you to harness: the shared desire to do great work. Although every dynamic is different, this urge consistently binds people together. And as the leader of an agency that's about to evolve – dramatically or more subtly – you can use it as rocket fuel to power your progress.

Interestingly, this shared motivation is particularly apparent if your leadership team is misaligned. Prior to running Market of One workshops, I'll often conduct one-to-one interviews with the senior stakeholders. As part of my briefing, CEOs occasionally warn me about two senior players who don't see eye to eye. 'Oh, watch out for Sandra and Stephen,' they might say, even expressing fear that the chasm between them can never be bridged.

I'm never worried when I hear this, even if the CEO is convinced that this interpersonal fracture might undermine the whole process. Once I speak to the Sandras and the Stephens, they always have far more in common than I was led to expect. Their typical desires include:

- Doing the best work of their careers
- Being proud of the brands they work on
- Earning decent money
- Building a brilliant culture
- Reaching the agency's potential
- Creating a space where everyone can thrive

- Doing the right thing – for their teams, clients and the planet
- Having a healthy blend of home and work life.

Of course the details vary, but it's remarkable how consistent these motivations are across agency shapes and sizes, disciplines and geographies. It's even more remarkable how powerful they can be once you harness them to create your Market of One.

Your rocket ship has all the fuel it needs.

Create the agency you'll love

Now that you've convened your group, they might still be a coalition of the curious and not yet a coalition of the willing. For that reason, you need to open their minds. As Albert Einstein probably never actually said: 'We can't solve our problems with the same thinking we used when we created them.' But it's a useful point to remember.

Change can't happen while it feels impossible. The sense of 'it's just how things are' or 'that won't work because' can be overwhelming. This is why the Big Grind is so habitual. So to prepare you for creating your Market of One, here are two thought exercises to loosen the ties that bind you to orthodoxy.

Exercise 1: Write your manifesto

Regardless of who owns your agency or how long it's been going, imagine that you're launching a shiny new independent. Like Gut, the Miami-based creative agency from Chapter 1, sit round the metaphorical kitchen table and write yourselves a manifesto.

Make big, bold statements of intent. Consider how you demand to *feel* on a daily basis. Edit out all the shit that brings you down. Fearlessly deploy absolutes like 'we will always' and 'we will never'. Describe your ideal clients. Define the work you truly want to do. Get clear on what fulfilment and commercial success really look like.

This simple exercise gives you permission to dream. Exploring what might be possible gets your coalition excited and energized. It's a great place to start.

Exercise 2: Design for abundance

The second thought exercise is to free yourself from the burden of needing to generate enough revenue to keep the lights on. Of course money is essential, but this is just an exercise. Specifically, what if you built the agency that you'll love, rather than one designed to be attractive to clients? It's made for you, not for them. What would that look like?

It might help to consider the difference between seeking a gap in the market or a market in the gap. The former speaks to a very narrow definition of success. It's about exploiting the gap before anyone else. Although this speaks to a speedy mind and a tidy profit, the opportunism can feel superficial.

Don't get me wrong, there's nothing wrong with nimble entrepreneurialism. If I was the bloke who first imported microscooters, I'd be sitting on a beach writing a very different book. But would I feel like I'd done my life's work? Probably not.

Contrast this with finding a market in the gap. This also speaks to seeing an opportunity, but here you start with what matters to you, rather than with where you can make money. It's about building the agency that you want to run and trusting that it will attract enough ideal clients to thrive.

This isn't some fortune cookie philosophy. Just slow down and listen for what inspires you. What kind of agency would you run if you knew it couldn't fail? What if you had total faith that success would happen, as long as you followed your passion?

PART THREE: Choosing to thrive

This is how the best agencies in the world think. They figure out what they're called to do and they go out and do it. It's not some supernatural talent that propels them, it's the exact same focus that you have access to. When it comes to sustaining commercial success, your conviction is a superpower.

Scale your excitement

With any luck, you're feeling excited. Whether the impetus for change originated with you or a visionary colleague, it's essential to come together as a senior team. And by applying your shared motivations of joy and fulfilment, you can quickly convene your coalition of the willing.

You're now ready to energize your wider agency as you apply the five principles and create your Market of One.

That just leaves one final piece to slot into the jigsaw – your mindset.

Chapter 12:
Enter the promised land

This book has invited you to consider a new perspective on running your agency. In amongst all the reframes and references to unwritten rules, there's one underlying change that's fundamental to creating your Market of One – the shift from a scarcity mindset to one of abundance.

It's sad to say, but scarcity thinking has become endemic in agencies. Risk aversion and self-limiting behaviours are so ingrained that they've long ceased being conscious choices. This perpetuates the Big Grind.

From clients and new-business to people and finances, making decisions from a fear of loss sucks the fun out of everything. Choose shit option A or *slightly less shit* option B? That's not a good day at the office.

But now that you've identified scarcity as the enemy, its grip on your consciousness can be released. In coaching we say that *awareness is curative*. Sadly that doesn't mean a blocker is removed just by seeing it. But it does mean that once you identify restrictive thinking, you can start understanding how it shapes your behaviours. And once you've done that, you can start making different decisions. That, my friend, is called *freedom*.

Rejecting scarcity means stepping into a world of abundance. This is a world where you make decisions from a place of curiosity. It's a world where everything happens *for* you, not *to* you. Positivity and optimism become the waters you swim in. Successes mean more because you're pursuing something meaningful. And occasional setbacks are simply welcome learnings along the way.

What it feels like in a Market of One

Creating your Market of One is to take charge of your future. Having a clear and lasting competitive advantage is your antidote to powerless commoditization. It's your gateway to a joyful life of abundance.

Once you have conviction about who you are and the specific opportunity you see in your market, a more focused business strategy becomes possible. This then enables you to develop a unique, ownable offer that your ideal clients will recognize as a clear alternative to your competitors.

This act of intentionality is transformative. Alignment is easy and your confidence becomes unshakeable. You're dedicated to client success, rather than filling your leaky bucket. Your work is world-class and the best talent is drawn to you. Doing the right thing is easy and profit naturally follows.

Nowhere is the contrast between fear and joy more tangible than in new-business. Having been the epicentre of scarcity, selling becomes your embodiment of abundance. Clients welcome your guidance because your rare expertise solves an urgent problem. You can promote, productize and price from a position of strength.

And now you're dedicated to *helping* rather than *persuading*, you can never 'lose' an opportunity – discovering that a fit is absent is no less a win than converting a pitch.

By reinventing how you sell, you're also transforming your client relationships. Because they're now based on expertise and trust rather than fear of loss, you can stand up for what you believe in – for them, as well as for you. This fosters mutual respect and shared success.

This is how embracing abundance and choosing to create a Market of One enables you to have the kind of growth, the kind of agency and the kind of life that you crave.

The future is yours

On the subject of choice, remember that fortune favours those who decide to act. Here's one final connection between conviction and commercial success.

As I was writing this book, I attended a conference in Madrid. One of the speakers was Nils Leonard, co-founder of the creative agency Uncommon Creative Studio. If you don't know Uncommon by reputation, then at least you'll remember their remarkable rise and eye-watering exit as one of the 'unicorn' success stories in Chapter 1.

Nils' keynote powerfully demonstrated how Uncommon delivers on its promise to 'build brands that people in the real world actually wish existed'.

The audience of agency leaders had heard just how pivotal this Proposition has been to Uncommon's startling success – especially how it doesn't just give them permission to do game-changing work, it means their clients literally demand it.

Given that Nils is smart, passionate and articulate, I asked him the million dollar question:

PART THREE: Choosing to thrive

> 'All agencies yearn to do ground-breaking work, and your Proposition bakes that expectation into what clients demand from you, so why don't more agencies create their own unique market in this way?'

His answer?

'I have no idea.'

I couldn't have put it better myself.

The future is yours. If you want it.

Appendices

Resources

Are you one of those people who likes to jump straight to the end of a book? If so, I'm afraid the big reveal was right at the start. But don't worry, here it is again:

The agency market isn't oversupplied, it's just under-differentiated.

Believing the former makes you a hostage to fortune. Embracing the latter means you can create your Market of One and change the world.

So what now? As first mentioned in Chapter 1, here are two tools from Co:definery that will help you on your journey:

1. **Business Case Calculator**: This highlights the commercial impact of creating your Market of One. Just plug in your current new-business performance numbers and play with the variables. Once you're seen as tangibly different by your ideal clients, you might be surprised at just how much more revenue you can generate.

    www.codefinery.com/bcc

2. **Market of One Diagnostic Questionnaire:** This helps you assess how well your agency currently follows the five principles described in the book. The Diagnostic Questionnaire gives you a tailored report that illustrates where you're strong, as well as where to prioritize change.

   www.codefinery.com/dq

Needless to say, if you'd like to discuss Co:definery's consultancy support to help you create your Market of One, we'd be delighted to hear from you. Feel free to get in touch via hello@codefinery.com

Similarly, if you'd like to explore how we can help you on a coaching basis – for individuals or teams – you can find out more at www.codefinery.com/coach

And if your conference or away-day needs an external challenge to the conventional wisdom around agency growth, you can book Robin as a speaker. For more information, visit www.codefinery.com/speaking

Finally, here's how you can stay in touch with our latest thinking:

1. **The Immortal Life of Agencies**: As liberally self-promoted throughout this book – #SorryNotSorry – this is Co:definery's podcast. It's all about creating more optimism around the future of the agency business. See what you think.

   www.codefinery.com/podcast

2. **Believe in Better**: As much as I can't bear the word 'newsletter', I've yet to think of a better description (all suggestions welcome). *Believe in Better* is our regular-ish newsletter that gives you priority access to our latest articles, podcast guests and the like. No-one needs more email in their life, but it's good stuff. I promise.

   www.codefinery.com/insights

Further reading

Introduction

4As (American Association of Advertising Agencies) and ANA (Association of National Advertisers) report. Available from: www.ana.net/miccontent/show/id/rr-2023-07-ana-4as-cost-of-the-pitch

Chapter 1

Barney, J. 'Firm resources and sustained competitive advantage' in *Journal of Management*, 17 (1): 99–120. 1 March 1991. Available from: https://journals.sagepub.com/doi/10.1177/014920639101700108

Blum, S. 'Liquid Death, the Canned Water Company for Hipsters and Head Bangers, Doubled Its Valuation Overnight' in Inc.com [online]. 12 March 2024. Available from: www.inc.com/sam-blum/liquid-death-the-canned-water-company-for-hipsters-and-headbangers-doubled-its-valuation-overnight.html

Graeme, N. 'The recipe for agency swagger.' Interview with Co:definery's The Immortal Life of Agencies [podcast]. 9 July 2024. Available from: www.codefinery.com/podcast_episode/episode-10-natalie-graeme/

Porter, M.E. *Competitive Strategy*. Free Press. 1980.

Spanier, G. 'Uncommon Creative Studio sells majority stake to Havas in deal worth up to £120m' in *Campaign* [online]. Available from: www.campaignlive.co.uk/article/uncommon-creative-studio-sells-majority-stake-havas-deal-worth-120m/1829588 [accessed 1 December 2024].

Chapter 2

Farmer, M. *Madison Avenue Manslaughter*. LID Publishing Inc. 2015.

Hemingway, E. *The Sun Also Rises*. Scribner's. 1926.

Levine, A. and Heller, R. *Attached: Are You Anxious Avoidant or Secure? How the Science of Adult Attachments Can Help You Find – and Keep – Love*. Bluebird. 2011.

Meikle, D. *Tuning Up: Improving Performance and Reducing Stress in Advertising and Marketing*. Lishakill Publishing. 2023.

The smiling curve. Concept first proposed around 1992 by Stan Shih, founder of Acer Inc. For more information, visit https://en.wikipedia.org/wiki/Smiling_curve

World Federation of Advertisers. Project Spring. Available from: https://wfanet.org/leadership/project-spring

Chapter 3

Hahn, G. 'The risks of malicious obedience'. Interview with Co:definery's The Immortal Life of Agencies [podcast]. 19 November 2024. Available from: www.codefinery.com/podcast_episode/episode-17-greg-hahn/

Klaff, O. *Pitch Anything: An Innovative Method for Presenting, Persuading, and Winning the Deal*. McGraw Hill. 2011.

Chapter 6

Kennedy, John F. Speech by John F. Kennedy to further inform the public about his plan to land a man on the moon before 1970. 12 September 1962. Available from: www.rice.edu/jfk-speech

Sullivan, D. 'How to Sell Transformation Using This One Question.' Strategic Coach [online]. Available from: www.strategiccoach.com/resources/the-multiplier-mindset-blog/how-to-sell-transformation-using-this-one-question

Sutherland, R. 'Where does innovation really come from?' Interview with Co:definery's The Immortal Life of Agencies [podcast]. 27 February 2024. Available from: www.codefinery.com/podcast_episode/1-rory-sutherland/

Chapter 7

Baker, D.C. *The Business of Expertise*. RockBench Publishing Corp. 2017.

Séguéla, J. *Don't Tell My Mother I'm in Advertising – She Thinks I Play the Piano in a Brothel*. Flammarion. 1992.

Sinek, S. *Start with Why: How Great Leaders Inspire Everyone to Take Action*. Portfolio. 2009.

Chapter 9

Allen, K. *Hidden Agenda: A Proven Way to Win Business and Create a Following*. Routledge. 2012.

Biblical reference: John 8:2.

Bonn, R. 'Stop paying agencies for their time and start paying for their output' in Marketing Week. 5 October 2020. Available from: www.marketingweek.com/stop-paying-agencies-time-start-paying-output/

Enns, B. 'Why We Suck at Negotiating' in Win Without Pitching [online]. Available from: www.winwithoutpitching.com/why-we-suck-at-negotiating/

Rackham, N. *SPIN Selling*. Routledge. 2017.

Chapter 10

WARC report. 'Global Ad Spend Outlook 2024/25: A Decade of Consolidation' in WARC [online]. Available from: https://page.warc.com/global-ad-spend-outlook-2024-25.html

Additional reading

Here are some other books you might enjoy as further reading. Although they haven't been directly referenced within these pages, they've certainly influenced my own learning journey over the years.

Bounds, A. *The Jelly Effect: How to Make Your Communication Stick*. Capstone. 2007.

Enns, B. *The Win Without Pitching Manifesto*. Gegen Press. 2010.

Fitzpatrick, R. *Write Useful Books: A Modern Approach to Designing and Refining Recommendable Nonfiction*. Useful Books Ltd. 2021.

Pease, A. and Pease, B. *The Definitive Book of Body Language: How to Read Others' Attitudes by Their Gestures*. Orion. 2017.

Rumelt, R. *Good Strategy, Bad Strategy: The Difference and Why It Matters*. Crown Currency. 2011.

Stanier, M.B. *The Coaching Habit: Say Less, Ask More & Change the Way You Lead Forever*. Page Two. 2016.

Williams, T. *Take a Stand for Your Brand: Building a Great Agency Brand from the Inside Out*. Copy Workshop. 2005.

If you enjoy these books too, please pay it forward and share them more widely.

Acknowledgements

They say it 'takes a village' to raise a child. Writing a book takes at least a town. So for your sake, I'll try and keep this brief.

But before I start the thank-yous, one last disclaimer to go with the three at the start. I've done my best to share my influences and acknowledge my sources, but it's possible that something might have slipped through. In my defence, it's a truth of human nature that once we embed a new learning, it can be hard to recall the world before that knowledge arrived. So this book may contain ideas or phrases that I've long since disconnected from their origin. If you spot anything, please let me know via hello@codefinery.com

Moving on to the people who've been instrumental in the conception and realization of this book, it's customary to end with the gushiest one, but I'm going to subject you to that first – even if its lavishness overshadows all subsequent thank-yous. So to my wife and business partner Inga, to say that without you there'd be no book feels criminally obvious. The value of your inspiration, perspective and incisiveness – in this book and everything we do – is impossible to put into words. You're in my heart and soul, and you're the spring in my every step.

For professional inspiration for as long as I can remember, thank you to Blair Enns, David Clayton, David C. Baker and

Tim Williams – each are unique and innovative voices. Seek them out and thank me later.

For their broader guidance and support, huge thanks go to Kevin Allen for his early mentorship; Keith Hatter for being a singular source of professional confidence; *Marketing Week* editor Russell Parsons for trusting me to learn to write; and the incomparable Hugh Baillie for always being right in the end.

Some other special thanks – for my friend, colleague and book recommender, John Monks, without whom I wouldn't be writing, coaching or married; for Nathan Anibaba for birthing – and naming – Co:definery's podcast; for creative polymath Cal Thompson for designing the cover and so much more; and for Charles Davies, whose wisdom shows up whenever it's needed.

Thanks to all of the guests on Co:definery's podcast *The Immortal Life of Agencies*, you help raise the bar for everyone – not least me, as the ideas in this book were refined through our conversations. Likewise, my immense gratitude to all those who listen and connect.

Turning to the book specifically, massive thanks to the teams at Practical Inspiration Publishing and their production partner, NewGen Publishing UK. Not all superheroes wear capes and I'm not sure whether you do or not, but your patience, expertise and guidance has made this book as good as it can be. There's no higher praise than that.

Particular thanks goes to Practical Inspiration head honcho, Alison Jones. Your advice to slow down and enjoy the process was profoundly valuable. Thanks also to Rosie Stewart, my development editor, for providing a wealth of good ideas to turn my first draft into something readable, and for my copy editor Lesley Cooper for guiding our final dip for the line.

To my kind and supportive beta readers who helped locate the book beneath the flab, I will be forever grateful – not least

Acknowledgements

because I know how busy you all are. Anyone who reads this finished product owes each of you a pint – and so do I. For now, thank you to Andrew Johnstone, Colin Barnhart, Greg Hahn, James Goldhill, John Harris, Lynne Collins, Marco Scognamiglio, Martin Barnes, Matt Simpson, Rebecca Vickery and Tom DiSapia. Special mentions for David Meikle, Laurence Green, Michael Farmer and Toby Southgate, whose generosity and insight went light years above and beyond. Thank you all so much.

Thank you to the contributors who were happy to lend their thinking to this book: Andy Pearson, Blair Enns, David C. Baker, David Clayton, David Wheldon, Greg Hahn, Kevin Allen, Sir Martin Sorrell, Natalie Graeme, Nils Leonard, Oren Klaff, Rory Sutherland and Russell Parsons. And a bonus hat-tip to Tracy Allery.

Thanks also to the wonderful authors (amongst their other talents): Andy Brown, Nikki Gatenby and Trenton Moss. Your generous advice on book writing and marketing is enormously appreciated.

Turning to you, the reader – without you, this book is just a paperweight. Along with Co:definery's clients, past and present, and the organizations, communities and trade bodies that have kindly offered us a platform over the years, I celebrate your optimism and commitment to discovery. Thank you for trusting me with your attention.

Finally, to Mum and Dad (the real 'Sandra' and 'Stephen'). Literally none of this happens without your unending love and support. Sorry you missed this, Dad. I like to think you'd have been chuffed.

About the author

Robin Bonn is the CEO of Co:definery, one of the world's leading consultancies specializing in agency positioning. Having spent 25 years driving growth for global networks, indies and start-ups across emerging and traditional disciplines, he has a deep understanding of what it takes to build a thriving agency.

Before launching Co:definery in 2016, Robin had a long career in agency growth, winning pitches for the likes of Spotify, P&G, Experian, ITV, Microsoft, Skype, Facebook and Ford. But as client challenges became more complex, he saw agencies struggling to keep up – clinging to outdated business models and so-called 'best practice' that no longer delivered.

Since then, Robin has been on a mission to de-commoditize agencies. A trusted advisor to some of the world's most renowned agencies – including global networks like DDB, UM, McCann and MullenLowe, as well as trailblazing independents like AnalogFolk, Stink Studios, VCCP and MSQ – he helps CEOs and founders reimagine what differentiation looks like, enabling agencies to scale faster, command a premium and attract the best talent in the industry.

Beyond consultancy, Robin is also an executive coach, a *Marketing Week* columnist, a founding co-chair of BIMA's CEO

& Leadership Council and a mentor for SheSays. He's served on the IPA's New Business Committee and the Direct Marketing Association's Agencies' Council. He also hosts *The Immortal Life of Agencies*, a podcast dedicated to fresh thinking and optimism in agency leadership.

Away from work, Robin is a proud dad of two daughters, a woeful runner, an amateur artist and a professional cat botherer.

Index

abundance mindset 5, 203–7
advocate's approach 173
ageism 43
Agency Customer Experience 135–9, 141
alignment 23, 149–51, 197, 206
Allen, Kevin 173
amateur selling 37–8, 39
anchor questions 163–4
artificial intelligence (AI) 40–1, 46
   evolving talent models 43
   holding company model 85
   pricing 178
authority, projecting 159

Baker, David C. 122
Barney, Jay 21
Bartle Bogle Hegarty 154, 135
Believe in Better 73, 77, 190
   avoiding inertia 80–1
   finding your spark 78–80
   hustle versus strategy 77–8
Berra, Yogi 191
best agencies 11–12
best practice, so-called 49–50
Big Grind 29, 190, 202, 205
   commerciality, lack of 35–40
   commoditized agency model 34–5
   how it developed 31–3
   inaction, long-term risks of 45–7
   oversupply symptoms 30
   urgency for change 40–5
Bigio, Gaston 18–19
Blandness Traps 55–6
boundaries 60–1, 160
budget, assessing client's 169–70
burnout 30
busyness and change resistance 193–4

capabilities 122–3
card sorting technique 172
change
   hurdles to 189–98
   need for 40–5
chemistry 37, 57–9, 160–1, 163
Chiat/Day 135
choice architecture 182
clarity 23
   Define your Dream 83, 89
   Narrative Hierarchy 107
   Walk the Walk 142, 147
Clayton, David 163, 171
client impact 22, 25
client-side procurement 32
coaching 149, 150–1
coalition of the willing 199–204
Co:definery 5, 7, 72
   Agency Customer Experience 135–9, 141
   Business Case Calculator 25, 38, 143
   coaching 149, 150–1
   Diagnostic Questionnaire 24, 194
   The Immortal Life of Agencies podcast 18, 61, 86
   Narrative Hierarchy 105–10
   Podium Test 95–100
   Rollout Masterplan 139–46
Coca-Cola 22
collaboration 199–204
commerciality 35–40, 161–2
commitment hurdle 198
commoditization 5, 14–16, 20, 34, 174, 176, 181, 206
   procurement pressure 43, 44
   reframes 51
   resistance to change 189, 191
   smiling curve 34–5

Appendices

competitive advantage 20–2, 71–5
confidence 23
   abundance mindset 206
   low 46
   Reap the Rewards 159, 172, 180
   reframes 57, 59
   unicorn agencies 18
conviction 95, 96, 100–1
costing 176–7
Covid-19 pandemic 79
Craft your Narrative 73–4, 103–4
   format 127–31
   Narrative Hierarchy 105–27, 144
   where not to start 104–5
curiosity 157–8, 163, 165, 206

Define your Dream 73, 83–4
   conviction 100–1
   destination 89–91
   distilling your vision 91–4
   exploring your ideal future 86–8
   leading without vision 84–86
   Podium Test 95–100
   Point of View 94–100
differentiation, deep 51–4, 133–9, 143
   resistance to 189–98
direction *see* Define your Dream
distinctiveness, superficial 51–4
diversity, equity and inclusivity 26, 42
Drucker, Peter 134

Einstein, Albert 202
empowerment 2, 5, 13, 22–3, 87
   reframes 49, 58, 60
Enns, Blair 158–9
enthusiasm, curbing your 159
excitement, scaling your 204
expertise
   promise of 106–9, 139
   proof of 106, 107, 109–10, 139, 154
   Reap the Rewards 154, 180
   reframe 56–9

Farmer, Michael 31
fear 55, 56, 193
features, advantages and benefits model 167
financial goals 84–5, 89
first impressions 162–4
fixed pricing 179–80
flexibility 130–1
fluffy aspirations 84, 85
focus 92, 149
Ford, Henry 77, 104
Franklin, Benjamin 139
friendliness 185–6

Graeme, Natalie 18
groupthink 88
growth
   Big Grind 30, 36–7
   clients' limited understanding 105
   nuances 79
   organic 25, 36, 71
   profitable 153
   reframe 50–1
Gut 18–19, 101, 135, 202

Hahn, Greg 61
Hatter, Keith 142
Hemingway, Ernest 45
How 106, 107, 109–10, 111, 112, 121–6, 129–30
hustle versus strategy 77–8

ideal future 86–8
   hurdles 91, 92
impact, prioritizing 140–2
implementation *see* Walk the Walk
inaction, long-term risks of 45–7
inertia, avoiding 80–1
inspiration 79–80
intermediaries *see* search consultants

jeopardy, assessing the client's 160–1, 181

killer questions 171, 172
Kit-Kat 22
Klaff, Oren 58
knowledge, deepening your 164–9

launch *see* Rollout Masterplan
leadership
   Define your Dream 91, 94–5
   no, saying 59, 61
   Reap the Rewards 186
   virtuous circle 23
   Walk the Walk 144, 147–9
leaky bucket 35–7, 46
Leonard, Nils 207–8
like-for-like, rejecting 180–1, 183
Liquid Death 17, 20

Mad Men 31, 39
manifesto 202–3
Marx, Groucho 66
Mead, Margaret 199–200
media commission model 31–2
Meh, Symptoms of 52–4, 63, 110
Meikle, David 42
meta questions 160
Mischief @ No Fixed Address 135
mission 149–51

Index

motivation 168–9

Naked 135
Narrative *see* Craft your Narrative
narrowness, concerns about 194–5
neediness, managing your 158, 159, 168–9
need-payoff questions 167–8, 171
new-business
 abundance mindset 206
 benefits beyond 25–6
 Big Grind 36, 38
 chemistry 57
 no, saying 59-61, 185
 performance 24
 virtuous circle 23
Nike 63, 64, 126
no, saying 59–61, 185

Ogilvy, David 92, 155–6
opportunity cost 25–6
optimism 2, 5, 8, 77–81
 abundance mindset 206
 artificial intelligence 41
 reasons for 90–1, 92
options, exploring 182–4
Oversupply Myth 2, 12–17
 Big Grind 29, 32, 33, 45
 reframes 49, 54
ownability 22, 101, 116, 117, 126

Partnership Delusion 38–40
passive mindset 15
payment terms 38, 160, 168, 169
Pearson, Andy 17, 20
performance indicators 142–3
performance-related pay 173
pitching 172–3
 Big Grind 36, 37, 44, 46
 effectiveness 65–6
 efficiency 24, 26
 hustle 78
plans, client's 165–7
Podium Test 95–100, 129
Point of View 94–101, 128–30
Porter, Michael 21
Positioning 106–8, 111, 114–16, 121, 129
 Carousel 64–6, 81, 107
positivity 206
premium, commanding a 176–81
pre-mortem 171–2
pricing 176–84, 193
 performance-related pay 173
priorities 167–8
processes 122–3, 124–5
procurement 43–5, 184–6

products as differentiators 138–9
profit 23, 26, 134, 176–81, 186
 Big Grind 30, 33
Proposition 106, 108–9, 111–12, 116–21, 128, 130

Rackham, Neil 167
Ramos, Anselmo 18–19
rapport *see* chemistry
Reap the Rewards 74, 153
 big reveal, ditching the 172–3
 budgets 169–70
 commerciality, reclaiming 161–2
 first impressions 162–4
 knowledge, deepening your 164–9
 leadership 186
 options, exploring 182–4
 premium, commanding a 176–81
 procurement, working with 184–6
 risk mitigation 170–2
 service, selling as a 157–61
 trusted advisor, becoming the 153–7
 value, selling 173–5
reframes 49–67
repitching 44, 46
reputational improvement 26
resource-based view (RBV) 21
risk mitigation 140, 170–2
Robbins, Tony 194
Rollout Masterplan 139–46

scarcity mindset 5, 50, 56, 168, 193, 195, 205–6
search consultants 37, 42, 60, 90, 145
Séguéla, Jacques 104
self-belief 5
self-care 147–8
service, selling as a 157–61
Shih, Stan 34
short-termism 85, 156
Sinek, Simon 129
size of agency 195–8
smiling curve 34–5, 41
Sorrell, Sir Martin 40–1
spark, finding your 78–80
specialization
 reframe 54–7
 resistance to 194–5
staff *see* talent
stagnation 86
Stella Artois 176
Stockholm Syndrome 39, 192
Straplines
 Narrative 106, 107, 111, 112, 114, 126–7, 129
 reframe 61–7

227

Appendices

strategy
  hustle versus 77–8
  reframe 61–6
  see also Craft your Narrative
subjectivity, embracing 174–5
success, focus on client's 154–7
Sullivan, Dan 87–8, 89, 90, 164–5
supplier conditioning 13–14, 159
Sutherland, Rory 86
Symptoms of Meh 52–4, 63, 110

talent 23, 26
  Big Grind 30
  evolving models 41–3
  retention 86
This is Spinal Tap 24
tiered pricing 182–3
time, and pricing 178
True & North 163–4, 166, 171
trust
  abundance mindset 207
  Agency Customer Experience 137
  Narrative Hierarchy 121–6
  Reap the Rewards 153–7, 162–3, 164, 169, 172, 175, 177, 179–80, 186
truth
  finding your 96–7
  Narrative Hierarchy 123–5

Twain, Mark 121
Tyson, Mike 198

Uncommon Creative Studio 18, 19, 135, 207–8
unicorn agencies 17–20, 135, 197, 207

value, selling 173–5
values 42
VCCP 56
vicious cycle 30
virtuous circle 22–4
Vision 113, 120, 196, 198
  distilling your 91–4
  see also Define your Dream
VRIN model 21

Walk the Walk 74, 133–4
  alignment 149–51
  depth of difference 134–9
  happy leader, happy agency 147–9
  Rollout Masterplan 139–46
Wheldon, David 178
Williams, Tim 177
World Federation of Advertisers 45
writing, power of 80

A quick word from Practical Inspiration Publishing...

We hope you found this book both practical and inspiring – that's what we aim for with every book we publish.

We publish titles on topics ranging from leadership, entrepreneurship, HR and marketing to self-development and wellbeing.

Find details of all our books at: www.practicalinspiration.com

Did you know...

We can offer discounts on bulk sales of all our titles – ideal if you want to use them for training purposes, corporate giveaways or simply because you feel these ideas deserve to be shared with your network.

We can even produce bespoke versions of our books, for example with your organization's logo and/or a tailored foreword.

To discuss further, contact us on info@practicalinspiration.com.

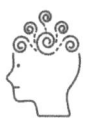

Got an idea for a business book?

We may be able to help. Find out more about publishing in partnership with us at: bit.ly/PIpublishing.

Follow us on social media...

- @PIPTalking
- @pip_talking
- @practicalinspiration
- @piptalking
- Practical Inspiration Publishing